THE TECHNIQUE
OF ACTING

STELLA ADLER

THE TECHNIQUE

OF ACTING

Foreword by Marlon Brando

BANTAM BOOKS
TORONTO • NEW YORK • LONDON • SYDNEY • AUCKLAND

THE TECHNIQUE OF ACTING
A Bantam Book / September 1988

Library of Congress Cataloging-in-Publication Data

Adler, Stella.
  The technique of acting.

  I. Acting. I. Title.
PN2061.A35 1988   792'.028   88-47514
ISBN 0-553-05299-3

Published simultaneously in the United States and Canada

Bantam Books are published by Bantam Books, a division of Bantam Doubleday Dell Publishing Group, Inc. Its trademark, consisting of the words "Bantam Books" and the portrayal of a rooster, is Registered in U.S. Patent and Trademark Office and in other countries. Marca Registrada. Bantam Books, 666 Fifth Avenue, New York, New York 10103.

PRINTED IN THE UNITED STATES OF AMERICA

DH   0 9 8 7 6 5 4 3 2 1

To my father, Jacob P. Adler,
and my mother, Sara Adler

ACKNOWLEDGMENTS

This book was written with the kind assistance
of Irene Gilbert and Mel Gordon.

I would like to express my appreciation
to the senior staff of the Stella Adler Conservatory
for their dedication to my work.

CONTENTS

FOREWORD

To me Stella Adler is much more than a teacher of acting. Through her work she imparts a most valuable kind of information—how to discover the nature of our own emotional mechanics and therefore those of others. It is troubling to me that because she has not lent herself to vulgar exploitations, as some other well-known so-called "methods" of acting have done, her contributions to the theatrical culture have remained largely unknown, unrecognized, and unappreciated. She was one of the very few, if not the only one, who went to Paris to study with Konstantin Stanislavski, who was a skilled observer of human behavior and a prominent figure in Russian theatre. She brought back to this country a knowledge of his technique and utilized it in her teaching. Little did she know that through her teachings she would impact theatrical culture worldwide. Almost all filmmakers anywhere in the world have felt the effects of American films, which have been in turn influenced by Stella Adler's teachings. She is loved by many and we owe her much. I am grateful to the inestimable contributions she has made to my life and I feel privileged to have been associated with her professionally and personally throughout my life.

Now she has written a book on acting that ably contributes to understanding the nature of this ancient, and apparently instinctive technique of representing ourselves to others in a manner that is now reflective of how we truly are. Perhaps a few brief comments about it would not be inappropriate.

The oldest profession in the world is not whoring, it's acting. This is not meant to be a pejorative comparison in any way. It is a simple fact that all of us use the techniques of acting to achieve whatever ends we seek, whether it is a child pouting for ice cream or a bawling politician bent on stirring the hearts and pocketbooks of potential constituents. Statesmen the world over would have amusingly short careers without the aid and judicious application of this craft of acting. Why the perception persists that there is a distinction between the professional actor and those of us who act naturally out of our daily needs is a puzzle. It is hard to imagine that we could survive in this world without being actors. Acting serves as the quintessential social lubricant and a device for protecting our interests and gaining advantage in every aspect of life.

Acting is a fascinating phenomenon of human nature, and Ms. Adler presents us with an analysis of the technique of acting that is incisive, intelligent, and long overdue. I hope that everyone is as pleased to read this book as I was.

—Marlon Brando

THE ACTOR AND THE PROFESSION

"Would that the stage were a
tightrope where no incompetent
would dare to tread."

—GOETHE

Goethe is, of course, speaking from an author's point of view. It
is the actor's tremendous and frustrating challenge to act in plays
written by Goethe and other great playwrights. Actors have to
communicate complex and subtle ideas, like those that appear in
Strindberg, Ibsen, Shaw, and Arthur Miller.

The modern actor must have virtues that the playwright,
perhaps, does not have, and one is the instinct that awakens the
actor to act. That instinct is stronger than we know or can
analyze. An actor's total being—mind, spirit, soul, and that unan-
swerable essence which is talent—must be devoted to his craft.
In this life, most people are forced to use only one side of
themselves. All those other selves create a unique unquiet in the
actor's soul, and that is what provokes the actor's talent to be
heard.

For over a century there have been many styles of writing:
Realism, Expressionism, Symbolism, and so forth. An author has
many years in which to explore these styles, past and present.
The young actor must make all these changes in style come alive
in the present. To overcome the hurdles, the young actor today
may look to an acting school, and this is perhaps the first step
that leads him to *the profession of acting.*

Often, the actor comes with no standards. In other periods
of the theatre, the novice was influenced by actors of great

talent. The novice entered the stage carrying a spear and, in this way, slowly learned his craft from the great ones, like Salvini and Kean. In more recent times, acting schools were often attached to theatres, and eventually the actor became part of the theatre. First they became actors—and then directors and teachers as well. The Moscow Art Theatre is an example of this.

The history of playwrights reveals their unbelievable knowledge; many have traveled, known paintings, literature, and music, and thus prepared themselves to write plays of distinction. And so most writers and scenic and costume designers have a through-line from the cultural past that strongly influences their work today.

In our moment in history, there are no standards for the actor, and often not for the teacher. Since the 1930s, all social rules for the actor have changed: his behavior, the way he dresses, his speech. All these facts have created an individualism in each actor that rules out the teacher's ability to judge him. The teacher knows that each actor comes without any values, and, in spite of this, a talent may lie dormant.

The actor of the present time has to be helped. Here, the teacher's influence is very specific. The teacher guides the actor as he begins to work with ideas. The explanation of the author's text, the behavior of the character, the style, the language, the play's rhythm—these awaken the actor to experience the life and style of the playwright.

Arriving at this awakening jolts the actor into realizing that his soul, his spirit, and his intellect have size. Just being an ordinary guy or girl is not enough. As we are today is not enough for the actor, and what is more important, not interesting for the audience.

The actor has in him the collective consciousness. It's as if all knowledge and all wisdom are contained in his mind. Through his vast imagination he inherits the wisdom of his ancestors without having had the personal experience. The actor, throughout history, has always had a deep and cosmic understanding. The teacher can now capture this understanding and release the actor's imagination. The actor can now grow and approach the life and style of many modern playwrights from Ibsen to the present.

The actor's imagination now takes in the character's life. He can deal specifically with the author's play, with the morality,

ethics, education, family life, sexual life, religious belief, and profession of the character. This approach gives the actor a control
and creates an inner security. The marriage of his mind with his
inner depth is the road to this independence in the profession.
His inherited, instinctive knowledge of human beings will always
come to his rescue.

THE IMPULSE TO ACT

Although the actor belongs to a very old and well-recognized
profession that goes back several thousand years, it has always
been difficult to define his place in society. He fits neither into
the middle class nor into the intellectual class, sharing none of
the commerical instincts of the former or the scholarly interests
of the latter. In a sense, the actor is in a class of his own, an
artist unlike other artists, who works uniquely with his body, his
soul, and his voice as his instrument. Yet, the place of the actor
in his own profession is clear and unchallengeable. On him rests
the high responsibility of interpreting the content of the play, of
bringing the ideas of the playwright to life, and of playing characters of such size as Oedipus, Hamlet, Hedda Gabler, Joan of Arc,
and Willy Loman.

It is not an extravagant claim to make that the actor,
because he is the interpreter, is the most important element in
the theatre. And so it is perhaps not surprising that a wide
variety of people from very different conditions, whose educational
qualifications and backgrounds are likely to vary widely, choose
acting as a profession. Differing radically even in their social
ideas, they are alike in their desire to become actors. While this
overriding desire to act may convince them that they *can* act and
they *will* become actors, they are likely to have crippling problems that make reaching their goals difficult, if not impossible.
Shyness, insecurity, and tension are common problems, as are a
lack of discipline, ignorance of tradition and manners, and no
sense of body control. Like lost souls, they may be frightened
and unconventional, yet ambition catapults them onto the stage.

So, let's start at the beginning. I will try to make everything
as clear as possible. Let me begin by saying that Konstantin
Stanislavski's system is a technique of acting, and techniques have

always existed. But his is the most modern technique, although it was discovered and formulated almost one hundred years ago.

The reason Stanislavski, the founder of the Moscow Art Theatre, created a new technique was out of a simple theatrical necessity: The old-fashioned styles of performance could no longer accommodate the new kinds of plays being written by Chekhov, Ibsen, Strindberg, and others.

In the United States, Stanislavski's system began to be known simply as "the Method." For some reason, his teachings quickly became distorted in America. Not by all actors, but by many. Gossip columnists and magazine writers furthered this misinterpretation until the average theatre-goer must have thought the profession of acting was made up of a bunch of inarticulate—and often slobbering—actors showing off their "real feelings," even when they had nothing to do with the playwright or his characters.

After having acted and directed in the American theatre, I had the chance to study privately with Stanislavski in Paris in 1934. I was stimulated. And when I returned to the United States, I wanted to share this extraordinary experience with other American actors.

While continuing to act, I started to teach and direct, trying to correct the mess that was made of Stanislavski's technique.

The craft of teaching must have a broad base. My teaching was and is based not only on Stanislavski's ideas, but also on a natural system that is available to anyone. Acting is stubborn work, necessitating constant attention and a rigorous schedule. It is not for geniuses. It is for people who work step-by-step. While there is no recipe for acting, it does follow a sequence of principles. The ideas and exercises that follow can work for you and give you the courage to fight for your development and craft.

First of all, you must see yourself as an artist, identifying and overcoming your faults.

It is easy for the young actor to start off badly. The skepticism of everyday life and loss of artistic ideals creates an environment of irreverance. Bad manners and smallness of scale and scope are the products of our times. It seems more difficult for the contemporary actor to discipline himself than it was for actors of previous generations. Actors frequently come smashed physically and emotionally. Therefore, their relationship to life is completely deadened. They seem to have no idea where they are or where they are going. But there is a basic need in human beings that makes them want to expand their personalities. There is a spark that wants to grow. That spark has to be kept alive. With much effort the actor can grow and graduate from callousness and emptiness into aesthetic maturity within a relatively short period of time. More important, with proper training you can stretch your talents immeasurably, creating a new depth and range of scenic roles.

On the stage, the actor is expected to create magic. He has to create a character that engages the audience night after night.

Spectators come for one reason only: to enjoy and fathom the human condition—to be jolted, to have an artistic experience.

More than anything, it is an actor's job to penetrate the playwright's creations—the subtleties and mysteries that the playwright's ideas contain.

The first concept an actor must master is a simple one. Acting means the elimination of human barriers. You must knock down the walls between yourself and the other actors. This will give you a sense of freedom on the stage.

The actor shows special generosity in saying to the audience:

"I am going to give you ideas."

"I am going to give you pleasure."

"I am going to dance for you."

"I am going to tell you the aches of my heart."

All of this is a form of artistry, of giving. It is a love affair with the audience. But, in order to carry on this love affair, you must begin to think and act in new ways.

There is a difference between the truth of life and the truth of the theatre. And you must learn not to mix them up. You are going to learn how to express yourself in size. You are going to express the author's epic ideas. The reason for this is that "Man is eternal," and he will be eternally struggling with ideas. You are a part of this eternal struggle. You must reach out. In the twentieth century, since our language is so modern, we do not feel our words. Our ideas are not put into words that interest people.

We live at a time in history when it is difficult to communicate ideas.

But the actor must communicate on the highest level. He must be the master of both words and ideas.

CHAPTER ONE

The Actor's Goals

The typical middle-class education is one of conformity. Rigid models of success and sobriety are placed before children from the very beginning. These set standards of behavior, or the Norm, are obstacles for the growing artist. This middle-class way of thinking (Norm) becomes a straitjacket for the imagination.

The dread of criticism, money madness, stage fright, unusual shyness, star dreaming, and character clichés are impositions made by the public. To be an artist you must overcome these obstacles. Everyday notions of good taste, beauty, and morality can mean death for *truthful behavior* and in-depth performance. People think they can act, but their thinking is often conventional. As an actor you must establish a new Norm—the actor's Norm.

One of the first jobs of the actor is to rid himself of outside opinions. Only when you respect someone more than anyone in the world can you accept and incorporate his opinions or criticisms. Otherwise, ignore people's notions of what is right for you. Nobody can tell you if you are young or old, beautiful or successful. These are ideas you must create for yourself. Most opinions on art and theatre are merely forms of gossip.

In my first session with actors, I always make a request: That each actor must carefully explain his (or her):

AIM: What is his goal and career plan?

Which comes first, **growth** (development) or **success** (money, fame, audiences)?

It is good for the young actor to verbalize his needs and fears, to make a distinction between people's (the public) idea of success (stardom) and the slow maturing of a great performer who can make more developed choices. In addition, the young actor has to have a strong awareness of himself and must be able to quickly list his assets and faults. An example of such a list is:

ASSETS	FAULTS
Desire for growth	Insecurity
Interest in reading plays	Procrastination
and background material	Untrained voice
Health	Poor diction
Good resonance chamber	Sloppy body behavior

Only with a true awareness of your qualities and faults and with daily work can you begin to learn and break out of your middle-class defensiveness. The young actor has to be reminded that his emotional range must be extended to the maximum. One cannot hold back on anything and be an actor. All this begins with self-awareness.

The actor has only his own body as an instrument. So write down what has to be fixed. As an actor you must work continuously on:

• your body
• your speech
• your mind
• your emotions

Your new Norm is clear: the will to survive. One's core must be made of steel. An actor has the right to survive, to grow as an artist. This entails a special strength, a new discipline, and self-awareness. Know what you want and have the courage to pursue it.

It is important to say aloud: "I am myself and have my own standards."

CHAPTER TWO

Beginning the Technique

The profession of acting gives the actor the opportunity to make of himself the most that he can be. The actor has the platform. He works with himself.

The ultimate aim of this technique is to create an actor who can be responsible for his artistic development and achievement.

ENERGY

Find the energy you need for your work. God doesn't give you this energy. And without it your work is boring.

Start with a large vocal energy; then you can modify it. The volume goes down, but the energy stays up.

Reading or speaking comes from the words on the page. The actor's understanding of these words must be clear and sharp.

EXERCISE #1

Energy of the Voice

1. Read an editorial aloud every day.
2. Read or speak ten, fifty, and a hundred feet away from someone to hear your true range.
3. Read as if the audience were across the table, across the room, across the street.

When you read aloud every day, you must hear yourself speak. In the passage you read, take out all the periods and commas. They keep you from speaking naturally, make your own punctuation.

REACHING THE AUDIENCE

Onstage, although you may be talking intimately to a partner, the audience must hear you as well, so you cannot use the private human voice you use in everyday life. You must reach your partner; you must reach the audience. Never communicate in a dead way. Your response must be articulate and personal. Young American actors today are inarticulate. You *must* have the facility to express the language.

Begin to have the awareness that everyone must hear you. Physically, you must reach the other person. Once you hear yourself projecting and sense the deep resonance coming into your voice, you will have found the normal tone to adopt on the stage.

When you are talking about big ideas, you cannot make yourself small. Your voice must resonate to the epic size of the playwright's ideas. Shouting the words is not necessary, but the ideas reach even beyond the audience. Your professional obligation from the stage is to make your partner and the audience understand.

When you have to communicate with a partner, put a space of six to twelve feet between you. This will discipline you to project your voice so that you will be heard during your rehearsals, and it will then carry over to performance. Get over using your everyday voice. This voice doesn't communicate. Being on a platform requires energy. Communicate with your partner without holding back. Communication will save your life.

TENSION

Tension is one of the absolute enemies of acting. You cannot use tension when you are on the stage. Tension is largely the result of going to the words of the play and depending on them, forgetting that the place and the action, rather than the words, are really the play.

When your attention is on the words, you worry mostly about yourself. Tension prevents you from being truthful on the stage, as you must be in speech and action or else you will lose the audience. But tension is reduced when your concentration is given to the actions. When you feel tension coming, locate the areas of tension. Relax those areas. Do it carefully.

You must be truthful in what you do or say. Feel the truth within yourself. The most important thing is for the actor to sense his own truth. The principle of using muscles is to use only the muscles that you need.

EXERCISE #2

Relax the whole body except one hand. Put all the tension into that hand. Sit and stand in that state.

PHYSICAL CONTROLS

PRINCIPLE: First you must achieve your norm and understand your body.

Physical controls must be located. As actors, you must learn to live with the physical controls until you can do them without thinking about them.

As an actor who is called upon to play many different kinds of people, you must learn to control your body so that you can perform movements you are not used to and develop different ways of walking that go with the character you are playing. The technique for doing this is to locate some physical alteration in your body—a stiff knee, for example, or a bent back—and locate it and the muscles that support and control it.

EXERCISE #3

Make a stiff knee. Control it by letting nothing else stiffen.

1. Walk with the stiff knee at home.
2. Walk up steps with it.
3. Dress with it.
4. Live with it.
5. March with it.
6. Dance with it.

If you do this for a few hours every day, you will be able to use this muscular control to play the part of a character who has a stiff knee. Be sure that this characteristic does not spill over and affect your other physical movements.

EXERCISE #4

Using only two fingers of your right hand, keep the second and third finger straight as if in a splint. Now:

1. Clean the table.
2. Put on your coat.
3. Take off your coat.
4. Put on a sweater.
5. Put on an apron.

This exercise will give you the ability to locate other parts of your body where you might need muscular control, such as a hip or a back.

You yourself must be convinced of the truth of what you are doing. You must learn to live with it constantly and also learn to forget it. The control must become second nature to you so that you are totally unconscious of it.

Control of your body and your voice are up to you. It is hard work to make yourself into an actor. When I worked with Stanislavski in Paris, he could not see me in the morning because every morning for two hours he would work on his voice in the attempt to overcome his slight tendency to lisp. Stanislavski was seventy-one at the time.

CONTROLS FOR SPEECH

Comparable to controls for the body are controls for speech.

Lisps

To affect a lisp, put your tongue at the back of your teeth and say the following sentence:

"She was a very stunning girl and she was walking up the street and she stopped to look at the shop window."

You must be able to locate where the lisp comes from. Learning the lisp is the beginning of learning how to manage accents.

EXERCISE #5

Practice lisps.

Accents

To get the accents:

1. It would be advisable to pick a vowel and two consonants of the language you are working on.
2. For languages and regional accents, we want you to use this control and practice it in your daily life until you are able to live with it.

EXERCISE #6

Practice a southern regionalism.
Practice a German accent.

MUSCULAR MEMORY

The moment you can use your hands and deal with imaginative props, you are in control of another principle in your work, the principle of the truth of the stage. You have learned the sensory truth of muscular memory.

Every prop has its own reality and truth.

- Fountain pen
- Pair of glasses
- Needle and thread
- Pair of scissors
- Sleeve with rip

The prop is always truthful. The actor must work so that he doesn't distort the truth of the prop.

The actor uses these props, combines them sometimes, and uses his imagination to make them truthful.

EXAMPLE:

- Eyeglasses, as a prop, are clean. But the actor, through his imagination, needs to clean them.
- The glasses are bent. The actor needs to straighten them.
- The glasses are broken. The actor has to fix them.

In every case, the actor has to use his imagination in dealing with the real prop as if it was in bad shape.

EXAMPLE:

- You must open a jar whose top has been fastened too tightly.
- You remember the muscular strength it takes to open such a jar in real life. Use it onstage.
- The lid on the jar is loose. Remember the muscular strength you needed to open the jar when the lid was on tightly.

The reality you create on the stage by threading a needle and sewing, or cleaning your glasses and putting them on, is not created so that the audience will believe in you; it is created so that you will believe in yourself. Histrionic acting is when you yourself are convinced of the truth of what you are doing. That is one of the essences of realism, and it is accomplished by doing very ordinary things.

You will learn from these exercises to use the sensory truth of muscular memory.

EXERCISE #7

To strengthen the skill of muscular memory, do the following:

1. Pick up the real needle.
   Thread it with imaginary thread.
2. Pick up the real thread.
   Thread the imaginary needle.
3. Use the real needle and thread to sew an imaginary hem on a small piece of material.

EXERCISE #8

1. Clean imaginary mud off your shoe.
2. Take off an imaginary feather from a real skirt or trousers.

EXERCISE #9

There is glue on your hand. Take one hand at a time, wash it, and see that each finger is clean of the imaginary glue.

ANIMAL MOVEMENT

The purpose of the animal exercises is to rid the actor of his social mask and to free him of his inhibitions.

EXERCISE #10

Take an animal you like. Be able to do the body movement of the animal and then add the sound the animal makes, but only after the movement is captured. Don't be afraid to make a fool of yourself. React as the animal would. Do this exercise for fifteen minutes each day:

1. Animal movements
2. Animal sounds
3. Bird calls

You will learn how you can use your body and voice differently.

EXERCISE #11

Put the animal in a place (circumstances):

1. Monkey in a zoo
2. Bear in a cage
3. Cat in the living room

CHAPTER THREE

Imagination

American actors greatly underestimate the wealth of their collective consciousness. If you are a typical American actor, then you have a faint sense of tradition. The United States has been alienated from the rest of the Western world, and so culturally, you have no relatives. You have dropped all tradition and sense of history. You have to place a greater value on your own store of knowledge and accept a higher personal appreciation of the self.

Ninety-nine percent of what you see and use on the stage comes from imagination. Onstage you will never have your own name and personality or be in your own house. Every person you talk to will have been written imaginatively by the playwright. Every circumstance you find yourself in will be an imaginary one. And so, every word, every action, must originate in the actor's imagination. Unless a fact passes through you, the actor's imagination, it is a lie. In studio classes, therefore, the most important exercises are those that have to do with the use of imagination.

COLLECTIVE CONSCIOUSNESS

Your imagination consists of your ability to imagine things you have never thought of. In order to do this readily, you must be made aware of how rich your memory is, for the collective memory of Man is such that he forgets nothing he has ever seen, or heard, or read about, or touched. You have relied on only a tiny fraction of what you know. But you know everything. It is all there. An emormous wealth of material exists in the mind of the actor, never to be tapped except in plays.

If you confine yourself only to the social moment of your generation, if you are bound within the limits of your street corner, separated from every object or period that does not contain your own experiences, then the result is a disrespect for the world in general and an alienation from anything that is not immediately recognizable as part of your everyday habits.

The importance of dramatic literature runs from the ancient Greek culture to the twentieth-century culture, i.e.:

- All the regional and national characteristics
     a. Accents
     b. Natural resources
- The shifting and changing styles
- The different periods of time
- The social levels of society
- The mores and morals of passing years
- The cut of clothing from generation to generation
- The different furniture
- The various sounds of music from the past

It is this social evolution that has changed the earthenware mug into a paper drinking cup—this historic size is your inheritance.

Your imagination is the key that will unlock this vast treasure house of material.

The imagination can alert the actor toward immediate reactions. He can see fast, think fast, and imagine fast. In exercises to stimulate the imagination, I look for instantaneous reactions from the actors to whatever objects they are working with. For the imagination to come quickly, all the actor has to do is let it happen.

SEEING IMAGINATIVELY

EXAMPLE:

- The fresh shirt—what was the color?
- In what position did it lie?
- What was under the shirt?
- The tie—what was the color?

- How wide was the tie?
- How were the handkerchiefs folded?
- Were there initials on the handkerchiefs?

EXERCISE #12

An actress left cleaned clothes in the dressing room on a hanger. See each article of clothing and describe it instantly.

- What color was the suit?
- How was the collar made?
- Where are the pockets in the suit?
- Of what material was the suit made?
- Where are the buttons?

EXERCISE #13

I ask actors to follow me imaginatively:

1. Go to the window and look out.
2. Do you see a balustrade?
3. The pigeon on the balustrade?
4. Look at the pigeon as it flies away and look at the mess.
5. Look down over the balustrade
6. See a grocery wagon and bags of groceries.
7. Look at the color of the wagon.
8. A child is skipping rope.
9. Look at the shoes she wears.
10. Look at the man who is pulling the wagon.
11. Look at the way he is dressed.

If the actors have been able to follow the images and create them, they will have a sketch of the street. Draw it on a piece of paper. In this kind of an imaginative scene, I am your author and you have followed me imaginatively.

EXERCISE #14

Now it is winter. Put on your winter clothes. Come and look out of the window.

1. Snow has fallen.
2. There is clean white snow on the balustrade.
3. Across the way in front of a private house is a wagon.
4. The bags of groceries are wet.
5. A garbage can on the sidewalk is covered with snow.
6. Look at the gutter.
7. An old geranium pot is cracked open.
8. Look into the pot.
9. On a pile of snow is an old banana peel.

Go back over the scene again.

Now that you have seen it, you can accept the imaginative scene. It is true for you. Imagination refers to the actor's ability to accept new situations of life and believe in them. From your imagination come your reactions to the things that you like and dislike. If you cannot do this, you had better give up acting. Your whole life will depend on your ability to recognize that you are in a profession where your talent is built on imagination.

SEEING AND DESCRIBING

The principle of seeing is to take in a specific image carefully.

• An apple tree
• A wooden fence
• A horse and wooden wagon

You must see images in your head vividly and accurately before you can describe them. Only then can you give them back and make your partner or the audience experience what you have seen.

Keep your eyes open and take in everything visually. When you describe something, it must be *seen* by you. The difference between reporting and taking an image in and giving it back is what makes you an artist. Every day you feed off the real things around you. On the other hand, plays feed you an imaginative situation in which it is your responsibility to make everything in the situation real.

FACTS VS. THE ACTOR'S WAY

The most common, inartistic way of observation deals only with cold facts and objects.

EXAMPLE: Facts

If I ask an actor to describe what he saw at the grocery store, and he says, "I saw some grapes, and pears, and bananas," then he makes a good banker, but not a good actor. He is seeing things like an accountant. He is stating facts.

You, the actor, must allow the objects to speak to you; then you can speak personally about what you have seen.

EXAMPLE: The Actor's Way

When referring to the fruit, the actor says, "I saw fantastic pears that were big but looked too expensive to buy. Then I saw those wonderful Malaga grapes, long and very sweet. There were also some of those big, blue grapes, and the baby ones, the little green ones. Those you can eat by the pound, and, by the way, they're very cheap." That's more the actor's way.

EXERCISE #15

Describe Ms. Adler's office imaginatively:

1. Make a drawing of all the objects that are in it.
2. Look at it.
3. Go over it alone.

Then it belongs to you, and you will never forget it. Now you can give it to someone else.

For an actor there are many ways of seeing:

• To see specifically
• To see rapidly
• To see what catches your attention
• To see everyday activities in life and place them in circumstances
• To see the simple, eternal scenes of human behavior and nature in its historical setting

---

EXERCISE #16

To See Specifically

Describe a stone.
This is my stone, taken from the park:

"I saw a great big stone in the park. It was gray and its surface was uneven. Around it there was grass, but patches of the grass were dead and had turned yellow."

In order to make the stone more vivid to your partner, you expand on what you see. Don't use fancy words.
Now, give me *your* stone.

EXERCISE #17

Describe a rose.
If you say, "I saw a rose," and tell your partner about it, you must expect your partner to see your rose.
If I speak about a rose, the image of the rose is very specific.

"I saw a rose. It is red and yellow and has a long green stem with thorns on it."

Now the rose is not just a fact. It requires a certain energy to make your partner see what you see. For you alone to see it is not enough. Make it part of your technique to give these images to your partner.

EXERCISE #18

To See Rapidly

Certain exercises enable an actor to strengthen his powers of seeing. One is a familiar concentration exercise:

Go to a supermarket to the produce section.

1. See as much as you can in ten seconds.
2. Write down what you have seen.

Look at your partner.

1. See as much as you can in five seconds.
2. Look away.
3. Write down what he or she is wearing.

Look around the room.

1. Count to five, look away.
2. Call out ten objects you have noticed.

EXERCISE #19

To See What Catches Your Attention

1. A man climbing up a tree
2. A leaf falling from a tree on Fifth Avenue

Now "take" ten things that attract your attention and explain why. (If an image leaves you dead inside, don't take it. Go to the next one.)

EXERCISE #20

To See Everyday Activities in Life and Place Them in Circumstances (The Place)

1. Buying groceries (in a supermarket)
2. Clearing the table (in the dining room)
3. Vacuuming the floor (in an office)

In what specific circumstances are you seeing these activities?

EXERCISE #21

To See the Simple Eternal Scenes of Human Behavior and Nature in Their Historical Setting

There are actions of Man today that have existed throughout history. Things you see every day and don't notice have a historical life.

As an exercise, write down twenty actions that will last forever such as:

1. A man playing with a dog
2. A woman wheeling a baby carriage
3. A man buying a newspaper
4. A boy and girl holding hands
5. A woman carrying a laundry basket

Actors must exercise their powers of observation. You must be continually aware of the ongoing changes in your social world. Keep a journal filled with lists of observations. Don't describe mechanical objects such as light bulbs or radios or dishwashers. Go to things that are forever, like a particular tree or a particular flower. The tree has a certain size that makes it worthy of your description. Describe a leaf in different seasons.

There are writers and artists from all over the world who go to see the trees in season in the south of France; in New England.

EXAMPLE:
Most of the time, we take what we see for granted.

- That's a table.
- That's a chair.
- Those are bees.

In doing so we demean life.

EXAMPLE:
A husband and a wife go on a trip together.
He might say: "My God! That's Notre Dame!"
She replies: "Yes, I know."

• He sees the magnificent architecture of Notre Dame.
• She sees the fact.

They are seeing Notre Dame differently.

As actors, you must come to realize that each item you see is unique. You must be distinctly aware of everything you look at and make each thing live so that you can give it back to your partner.

You should not use too many words, and only those you like. The feeling evoked by the description is more important than the description itself.

EXERCISE #22

See how the sky looks at dawn; at midday; at midnight.

EXERCISE #23

Carefully observe colors.

1. See five different reds:
    • Apple red
    • Blood red
    • Rose red
    • Sunset red
    • Balloon red
2. See five different whites, blues, etc.

Each color is related to the object; that's what makes it alive in you.

At night before you go to bed, write down what you have seen during the day.

An actor should practice some variation of the above exercise daily. You have a responsibility to cultivate your powers of observation—by noticing people, by noting what they wear, by never walking along the street without noticing signs, store windows, people, animals.

In his letters, the celebrated American novelist Thomas Wolfe wrote: "This week I'm looking at noses. That's good."

EXERCISE #24

Go imaginatively to:

1. A boy being beaten by a policeman
2. A crowd that is breaking windows
3. A car where the wounded people are being taken out by the police

Use your imagination. These situations demand strong reactions.

Some actors hold back and do not react. Actors should consciously take things that will make them react. *In your choice is your talent.* Acting is in everything but the cold words.

Often an actor will protest, "I have a fear of pushing." He is afraid of forcing his emotions, of expressing more than the occasion and the circumstances call for. I say to you, do not push, but be able to let go. We have been so deadened by television. If your reluctance to push inhibits your reactions, you are too fearful of having feelings. If you push your feelings down long enough, you will eliminate them. Rather than having a false honesty, I would prefer you to make the extra effort.

From now on your work will lead you to live imaginatively. You will see and act in imaginative circumstances. This is not hard if you accept that everything you imagine is truthful. The actor's job is to defictionalize the fiction. If you need a lemon tree but have never seen one, you will imagine some kind of lemon tree. You will accept it as if you have seen it. You have imagined it, therefore it exists. Anything that goes through the imagination has a right to live and has its own truth.

EXERCISE #25

While walking along a country road:

1. Know where you are.
2. Look at the sky. It is absolutely blue. White clouds are drifting by and birds are flying in formation.

3. Along the fence is a meadow and in the meadow is a cow.
4. Look at its color.

Tell me three or four things that make the cow logical and real.

EXERCISE #26

Now you are walking down a lane:

1. The long branch of a tree has been cut off.
2. Throw it off the road.
3. Go up a small road.
4. On both sides the grass grows quite high.
5. You come to an old wooden bridge and a pond.
6. Lean over the wooden bridge.
7. In the pond is a school of tiny fish.
8. Farther down the road and across the pond is a yard with a clothesline tied between two trees.
9. Some clothes are hanging from the clothesline.
10. A child's pajamas, socks, sneakers
11. An old kitchen tablecloth
12. Overalls
13. Look at the overalls.
14. Notice their shape.

Ask yourself:

1. How tall was the grass on both sides of the lane?
2. How was the bridge made?
3. Where are the tadpoles?
4. Describe the sneakers?
5. The tablecloth?

What you have seen is now entirely yours.

In a play, the playwright is never going to give you a tablecloth that belongs to you. His script will simply say "tablecloth."

You will have to imagine that it is:

- Threadbare or fresh
- Wrinkled or starched
- Washed or dirty

The playwright will indicate only what it is. You will have to make it come alive.

If the playwright writes that the day is fine, you will have to give us:

- A sky that is blue
- White clouds
- Birds flying in formation

The discovery of what is fine about the day will be up to you.

The playwright is never going to give you a country road that belongs to you. He will only give you words that say, "I was walking along a country road."

You will create the road, saying to yourself:

- It is dusty.
- The color of rust
- There are cornfields on both sides.

Although the playwright indicates the circumstances, he does not give them to the actor.

As you imagine this scene, there will be many facts. Don't leave them dead. Realize through your imagination the life of each fact. As actors, you must create for us the miracle of life, not the fact. This life is what is called "the actor's creation." If you can create the play, you will know why you want to act. If you don't create it, you will not want to act.

The actor is like a writer, full of impressions that speak to him. He does not go around being a sort of clerk without a job, saying, "I'll have bacon and eggs." When the actor gets bacon and eggs, he sees:

- The waitress
- The table
- The restaurant with its rushed activity

The actor takes everything in. He is able to see that:

- The floor has dirt on it.
- The table is spotless.
- The coffee is weak.
- Nobody is really paying any attention to each other.
- Everyone is in a hurry.

He is not there just to eat, pay his check, and go out. He is able to live there, watching, seeing, understanding, by saying, "What is it? What is the place I'm in?"—the way a painter does, the way a writer does.

As you do these exercises, your confidence will increase. You will feel enriched by your ability to know that you can experience anything. You need to grow independent, and the ability you gain through these exercises will give you confidence and size.

CHAPTER FOUR

Circumstances

THE TRUTH OF THE PLACE

In life, every human being knows what place he is in. It is a given truth that everyone is somewhere. The place is called the given circumstances of life:

- In a pool
- On the beach
- In the library
- In school

All people are great actors because they accept exactly where they are. Actors, however, are often terrified of the stage because on the stage they feel abandoned in a place that is foreign to them. Suddenly, they are in the play's circumstances and that is what is so foreign to them. They are left without the absolute security that a familiar place gives the actor. When they go out on the stage they see nothing. It is as if they were blind. In order to avoid this, actors must immediately make clear to themselves the circumstances of the play that is taking place on the stage.

First the actor must begin to recognize objects, furniture, and the features of the setting. Before he goes to the text, it is imperative to physically move around in the new circumstances and use them. For example:

- Sitting on the couch
- Opening a door
- Looking out the window

Until this facility is gained by the actor, he will be lost.

The time he gives to accustoming himself to the set, which is now a specific room or garden, will give him the relaxation, the sense of truth, and the self-confidence that he needs to start on a new script.

If actors are not comfortable in the space, they cannot work. Unless they can achieve the relaxed behavior that will allow them to see the objects that belong in the environment and to react to them, they are wasting their time. Actors must familiarize themselves with the circumstances.

Stanislavski said, "The truth in art is the truth of your circumstances." *Circumstances* is the term we would like you to use as part of the vocabulary of acting. "Where am I?" is the first question you must ask yourself when you go onstage. Walking on the stage to locate the imaginary setting makes you feel at home. It also takes the tension out of the performance. Relaxation comes from your recognition of the truthfulness of the circumstances. Onstage, you are never actually in lifelike circumstances, but you have to accept them as such.

In most cases, the actor feels tension because he goes first to the words. The words do not make the play. You must understand that the first rule is that you accept the circumstances that the playwright gives you as the truth. If you work for twenty years on a play without knowing your circumstances, you will fail. If you go first to the words, you will not be a modern actor—just a bad one. As an actor you are always in given circumstances. It is your responsibility to fill that place. Take the fiction out of the circumstances by letting the place tell you what to do.

The complete absorption of the actor in the circumstances has another enormous benefit. If you pay attention to the circumstances, you will ignore the audience and not worry about people watching you. If you ignore them completely and just pay attention to what you are doing, they will love you.

If you really act, the joy is in the doing of it. If you accept the circumstances of the play and the partners that you have to deal with, the audience will be with you completely. The actor has much more fun living in his given circumstances than the audience does in watching. Any good actor who is on the stage and knows what it is like to experience the circumstances would not trade that experience for any other.

LIVING IN CIRCUMSTANCES

EXERCISE #25

If the space on the stage is a library, you walk around the stage establishing various areas of your library.

1. Books would surround you.
2. Where would be a place you would sign in? You would need to establish that area.
3. In the library there is a person more important than you—the librarian. Establish her area and keep your own area separate from hers.
4. If you use the library, what section would you go to? There would be a place for reference books, for poetry, for atlases, and so forth.
5. Select the area you would work in.

Now that you are in the circumstances, you are ready to deal with the script which will give you the actions and the dialogue. But remember that the circumstances will always come first.

The ideas of the great playwrights are almost always larger than the understanding of most actors, and you should look for these ideas. If you can identify with these ideas, then you share them with the playwrights. Your job now is what we call "interpretation." That is your interpretive responsibility.

A great disservice was done to American actors when they were told that they had to experience themselves on the stage instead of experiencing the circumstances. You must not take yourself and put that into Hamlet. Hamlet is a royal prince of Denmark. Therefore, the truth of the character is not found in you, but in the circumstances of the royal position of Hamlet, the character you are playing. The action of Hamlet—to decide whether to live or to die—has to be put in his circumstances, not in yours. The truth is always the truth in the circumstances of the character.

EXERCISE #26

You must be able to do actions in different circumstances. The action remains the same; the circumstances are different.
Your action is to dress:

1. Dress in a dressing room in a theatre.
2. Dress in your bedroom.
3. Dress in the locker room in a gym.

EXERCISE #27

In the circumstances of a restaurant, your action is to order dinner:

1. Go to the bar to get a drink.
2. Get to the table and order dinner.
3. Go to the check room and get your wallet.

EXERCISE #28

Using the circumstances of a shop, your action is to buy a blouse:

1. Pick a blouse from the rack.
2. Try it on in the dressing room.
3. Pay the cashier.

BUILDING THE LARGER CIRCUMSTANCES

- Where does the action take place? In a house
  - a. When? 1948
  - b. What time of day? 7:00 P.M.
  - c. What season? In the spring
- Build a place for yourself.
- Begin to live in the place as the character.
  - a. What does he do in this place?
- Every action has circumstances and is surrounded by larger circumstances.

a. What city/town? Boston, Massachusetts
b. What country? The United States
c. What hemisphere? Northeastern part of America bordered by the Atlantic Ocean

MOOD IN THE CIRCUMSTANCES

Mood comes from your circumstances. You get the mood out of each scene or act of a play. All circumstances have moods.

EXAMPLE:

• A church has its mood.
• A bar has its mood.
• A walk in the park has its mood.
• A hospital has its mood.
• A playground has its mood.
• A cemetery has its mood.
• A parade has its mood.

Your action can be light or dark, depending on the circumstances that the playwright has written about. If it's a comedy, it's light; if it is drama, it's dark; or it can be, in between, medium. The mood can change, and the playwright can shift the scene to include various moods.

CHAPTER FIVE

Actions

The aim of your approach to acting is to find the actions in a scene or play. The actions must be do-able, and they can be expressed by using the verb form.

- An action is something you do. To read.
- An action has an end. I'm reading the newspaper.
- An action is done in circumstances. I'm reading in the subway.
- An action is justified. I'm reading to follow the stock market.

STRONG AND WEAK ACTIONS

There are strong and weak actions. In order to be strong, an action needs an end, or objective. For example, I am going to leave the room. The room is the end of the action and the ending makes it strong.

I am going to write. This is an action without an end and is therefore weak. If your action is "to go away," it is a weaker action than "to go home."

STRONG ACTION	WEAK ACTION
I'd like to drink coffee.	I'd like to drink something.
I'd like to take a walk in the park.	I'd like to go somewhere.
I'd like to go to bed.	I'd like to rest.
I'd like to write a letter.	I'd like to write.

Let's start with simple actions.

The action is:

• To count <u>the lights</u>
    a. To count the lights in the chandelier
    b. To count the lights in the lamps
    c. To count the lights in the wall brackets
• To find <u>my bag</u>
    a. To find my bag on the floor
    b. To find my bag in the closet
    c. To find my bag in the room

The previous examples are of actions that have a definite ends and are done in circumstances. What is underlined will make you aware that the end gives you the meaning in each action. These are simple actions which are connected to larger actions.

EXPLANATION OF AN ACTION

In an Action, You Must Know:

• What you do. Have dinner
• Where you do it. In dining room
• When you do it. At dinnertime
• Why you do it. To feed the family after work

But you don't know how you do it. The how is spontaneous and unexpected. The action never includes the how.

EXAMPLE:

Action:

• Cleaning the office	**What** are you doing?
• Special room in apartment	**Where** are you doing it?
• Nine o'clock in the morning	**When** are you doing it?
• Two clients are coming for a meeting	**Why** are you doing it?

NATURE OF AN ACTION

Every Action Has its Nature.

- To put on shoes
- To put on socks
- To iron napkins
- To arrange drinks
- To dress the doll
- To sort your mail
- To sort the bills

Every action you do has its *nature*. That means its truth. In order to be truthful onstage you must know the nature of what you are doing and it must be truthfully done.

In some actions you *do* physical things. The things you *do* to accomplish your actions are called "activities."

Action: To Set the Table

- The nature of the action is putting out knives, forks, and spoons. These are what we call "activities."

EXAMPLE:

Action: To Set the Table
Activities:
- Put down glasses
- Put down plates
- Put down forks

EXAMPLE:

Action: To Build a Fire
Activities:
- Get the wood
- Get strips of paper
- Get lighting fluid

EXAMPLE:

Action: To Have Dinner
Activities:
- Pass the soup
- Cut the vegetables
- Mix the gravy

Once you have physicalized these actions (in the above examples), the *overall action* is "to spend the evening at home."

OVERALL ACTION (RULING IDEA)

All the techniques you have learned so far serve only one purpose, and that purpose is for the actor to arrive at what Stanislavski called the playwright's ruling idea.

Every character must move in the direction of the play's ruling idea. It is the duty of the actor to grasp its meaning. This is why the playwright writes the play.

The actor must be sure that the ruling idea of a given play appeals to him emotionally and intellectually. The actor must know how to make this idea his own. All the actions within a play are interconnected, and they all lead the actor to the ruling idea or overall action.

The author writes the play to be acted. But the playwright does not make the actor aware of how the play must grow to realize its ultimate meaning. Let us now explore this growth for which the actor is responsible.

An action should be broken up into smaller actions or steps. For example, in the action of going to work in the morning, there are a number of steps, such as waking up, eating breakfast, catching the train, etc. The overall action of going to work might be, *to keep the family together.*

EXERCISE #29

Complete the following action:

To Prepare Breakfast
Be sure and break it down into activities like:

1. Frying eggs
2. Squeezing orange juice
3. Buttering toast

PRINCIPLE: Steps in Actions:

- If an action is too complicated, divide it up into two or three steps and each step will help the growth of the action.
- Whatever steps you take in your action must be for and needed by your action.

Steps in an Action:

If your activity is to drink the coffee, you can do it. If your activity is to take off the ring, you can do it. But you cannot do the action to arrange a party, to go to work, or to go to Europe unless you break it down into steps that will add up to the action.

It would be helpful for you to write down, as it is written below, your action, the steps in that action, and the activities:

EXAMPLE:

ACTION   STEPS

To go to work   **Step 1.** Dress (The activities or nature of which is to):
Activities:
a. Change shoes
b. Put on earrings
c. Arrange pocketbook
Step 2. Have breakfast
Activities:
a. Put bread in toaster
b. Get coffee from kitchen
c. Fix cereal
Step 3. Arrange my business portfolio
Activities:
a. Sort mail
b. Look through lawyer's folder
c. Sign letters

Your steps are taken from the action. Stay with the action—feed off it.

EXAMPLE:

ACTION	STEPS
To prepare for a party	**Step 1.** To get my clothes together **Activities:** a. Choose a dress b. Choose a pair of shoes c. Choose a pocketbook **Step 2.** To prepare the drinks **Activities:** a. Put out the liquor bottles b. Get the ice c. Put out the glasses

These would all be part of the nature of "preparing for a party." Try not to choose more than three activities.

EXERCISE #30

Action: To leave for the summer
  Steps:

1. Pack your things
2. Check your money and passport
3. Leave a note for the maid to take care of the house

Action: To celebrate Christmas
  Steps:

1. Wrapping the presents
2. Trimming the tree
3. Addressing the cards

Do the activities or nature of each step.

PHYSICALIZING (DO SOMETHING PHYSICAL)

When I ask an actor to physicalize his actions, and use his circumstances, the purpose is to take the burden off the actor. If you read something in the newspaper that you like, tear it out. Then you will be physicalizing the action of reading the paper. You always have to keep the circumstances truthful. In life, as on the stage, not "who I am" but "what I do" is the measure of my worth and the secret of success. All the rest is showiness, arrogance, and conceit. Anything you do is physicalizing. Doing means physicalizing.

If an actor fails to protect himself on the stage by physicalizing his acting, we are likely to catch him attempting to act feelings. Instead, choose something physical to do like:

- Picking up a letter
- Putting the keys away
- Seeing that the lights are on

The mood of the play will be there, but not the truth of the play. Onstage, when truth comes in, we should forever celebrate it.

COMPLETING AND NOT COMPLETING ACTIONS

You either complete an action or you do not. If you do not complete your action, you must change it to another action. If you can complete your action, continue with it and then go into another action. But you must always be in actions—as opposed to being in words.

EXAMPLE:

a. **Action:** To go to the theatre
   (You've lost your tickets.)
   You cannot complete your action. You turn to an alternative action.
b. **Action:** To spend the evening at home

EXAMPLE:

a. Action: To take a bath
   (There is no hot water.)
   You cannot complete your action.
b. Action: To dress instead

EXAMPLE:

a. Action: To go to the theatre
   (The doorbell rings.)
   The action is interrupted.
b. Go to the action of welcoming your guest.
c. Go back to the original action of "going to the theatre."

Life can intrude on your action.

EXAMPLE:

Action: To study anatomy
Life intrudes on the action.

- The telephone rings.
- You close the window.
- You turn off the radio.
- You adjust the clock.
- You get a cup of coffee.

Always go back to your action of studying anatomy.

Example:

Action: To fix coffee

- The mailman rings the bell.
- The telephone rings.
- The supervisor wants to check the lights.
- The dog is scratching to go out.

Continue action of fixing coffee

ACTIONS WHICH DO NOT USE TEXT

There are actions which provoke you to use the circumstances, which do not use text.

EXAMPLE:

Action: To sew in my room

- I see a towel on the bed. Hang it up.
- I hear the taxi honking. Look out the window.
- I see my pocketbook. Get up to put money away.
- I see a drawer open a little. I get the sweater out.
- The clock rings. I check the time.

EXAMPLE:

Action: To read on the veranda

- Push your chair away from the sun.
- Add water to the flowers on the table.
- Get a pen from the table.
- Move away from the bees that are around you.

PREPARATION AND COVERED ENTRANCES

Whenever you enter or leave the stage, you go into specific circumstances, and you must prepare. Preparation is something you do for yourself.

Preparation is meant to help you start your action. It will also bring you closer to the given circumstances.

- Preparation is not another action.
- You must pick out the detail, the tiny thing that will help your action.
- Preparation is something you do for yourself.
- You take one thing from your circumstances that will help you start your action.

If your action is to enter the library, take some physical activity, such as taking off your coat or looking through your notebook, to help you across the entrance. When you come from one room into another, we need to know what room you've been in and what room you're going into. If you come in with fresh-cut flowers and put them in a vase, we may infer that you have just come from the garden. The preparation will keep you from tightening up. The prop will keep you truthful.

EXAMPLE:

Entering into:

• Office	Hold the mail while coming in
	Put eyeglasses away
	Use key to open office
• Bedroom	Take off scarf
	Put key back into purse
	Read name and address on letter
• Classroom	Take off coat
	Take off gloves
	Arrange class papers

EXERCISE #31

Bring in five preparations for an action.

ACTION: To hide
"He's looking for me, so I'd better hide."

Do something as you come in. Finish it on the stage. That way the audience can tell what you were doing before you entered.

Too many actors start off passively, not being in a specific place, without having that necessary physical preparation to push themselves into the action of coming into the room.

PAIN AND DEATH

Sooner or later in your work in the theatre, you will be called upon to express pain or shock, or you will be shot and have to die in full view of the audience. These are actions that cannot be experienced directly on the stage. These are actions for which you need a task. In this technique the words "as if" are used to stimulate you.

EXERCISE #32

Pain

If the character has a terrible headache, you, as the actor, must locate where the headache is. Then you can imagine it is "as if"

1. Someone were pushing in your eyeballs.
2. You were making a hole in your eyes.
3. I were sticking a needle into your eye.
4. I were pouring strong alcohol into it to clean it.

You must not work for the reaction. It must come at once from the image, and you must choose an image that affects you instantly so that this can happen.

EXAMPLE:
If you have a terrible toothache:

- Locate the place of the pain and then it is "as if" someone were scraping your gums with a razor.

Do not anticipate the pain. It must come from the razor scraping the gums. The use of metaphor to call up the reaction is not more than we do in real life when we say, "I have heartburn" or "My back is breaking" or "My head is splitting." The image projects the pain of experience. It is "as if" I had an open wound in the top of my head and ammonia was being poured into the brim of the wound. The imagination awakened by the "as if" will give you a technique to experience pain in any part of your body.

Death

If you are shot, you locate the place where you have been shot; you can fall forward or you can leap from it. John Barrymore's reaction to being shot onstage was to leap three feet in the air. Falling asleep comes closest to dying—the relinquishment of consciousness. You begin to lose life, lose the world. First the will is no longer in control. You try to reach out, but you cannot. You continue to breathe, but you can no longer move. The senses begin to leave you—hearing, vision, taste; then the brain goes and the heart stops. In dying, you experience these successive stages of loss until you are gone.

EXERCISE #33

This is your first play and it has many elements that you have worked on up to this point.

I. PLOT:
A revolution has broken out in a Latin American village where a children's hospital is under fire. Gunfire can be heard. An American Peace Corps worker must cross the enemy border to get medical supplies because the lives of the children are at stake.

OVERALL ACTION: To save the children

II. ACTION: To get help

III. STEPS:

Step 1: Escape by getting across the border.
   a. Pass through enemy fire.
   b. Swamp with deadly snakes must be crossed.
   c. Overcome barbed-wire barricades and thick underbrush.
Step 2: Shelter yourself in mud hut.
   a. Read the muddied medical list.
   b. Remove barbed wire from your leg.
Step 3. Signal for help.
   a. Wave a flag.
   b. Get shot in crossfire.
   c. Fight against dying.

The purpose of this exercise is to show you how to use your craft and technique to work in difficult and changing circumstances and to follow the plot from beginning to end before starting to work on your character.

- Every action must be truthfully performed.
- You must move through changing circumstances.
- Everything you do or think must be clearly justified.

EMOTION

The actor's mind, heart, and soul are involved in his profession. Sometimes the mind takes over. Sometimes the soul is more involved. This brings up the question of emotion. The actor has enough resources within himself to get the emotion that he needs from the play, from the character. All the emotion required of him can be found through his imagination in the circumstances. The actor must understand that he cannot exist truthfully except in the circumstances of the play.

If the actor needs an action which he doesn't respond to in the play, he can go back to his own life, not for the emotion, but for a similar action. In your own personal experience, you had a similar action in which you had an emotional response. Go back to the action and specific circumstances you were in and remember what you did in those circumstances. If you recall the place, the feelings will come back to you.

If the actor has to pray to Zeus and finds this difficult, he can say, "I have at some time in my life prayed," and he can go back into his own life for the action "to pray," which is to reach out. If he arrives at this action from his own life and his personal circumstances, he must take from it only the do-able side of the action, "to reach out." Once he knows what is do-able in the action of praying, he must go immediately back to the circumstances of the play and reach out to Zeus or Buddha. If he builds the background of his play and justifies the action of reaching out, because the children are dying, they have no water, their tongues are swollen, there will be enough to give him the action of reaching out or "to pray."

The physical side of the action "to pray" is "to reach out." Using an action from your past is the only way in which your personal past can be brought into the play. To stay with your personal past, which made you cry or gave you a past emotion, is false, because you are not now in those circumstances. You are in the play, and it is the circumstances of the play that have to be done truthfully by borrowing what was physical in the action you had in the past, not the emotion.

CHAPTER SIX

Justification

First comes the action, then a reason for doing it: this reason is called justification. Finding reasons for everything you do on the stage keeps your actions truthful. The creative part of your work, justification, is what you live off in the theatre.

The justification is not in the lines; it is in you. What you choose as your justification should agitate you. As a result of the agitation you will experience the action and the emotion. If you choose a justification and experience nothing, you'll have to select something else that will awaken you. Your talent consists of how well you are able to shop for your justification. In your choice lies your talent.

Justification can be done in many ways. Let's start with *instant justification*.

INSTANT JUSTIFICATION

This justification gives you the immediate need for what you are doing.

EXAMPLE:

Why are you opening the window?

- There was a crash outside.
- To get fresh air

Why are you closing the window?

- The shade was rattling.
- To keep the flies out

Why did you close the dressing room door?

- I was changing my clothes.
- The hinge was loose.
- I needed the stone that was keeping it open.
- To surprise people with my new costume
- To keep out the music of rehearsal

In the last example, the five answers serve as a spontaneous justification for the action of closing the door. But you can't say, "I closed the door because there was an actor in the hall I didn't want to see." This is an example of what we call adding fiction to the justification. A person whom you know nothing about has been brought needlessly into the picture, and instant justification goes out the window.

EXAMPLE:

Why are you getting dressed?

- I'm changing for the second act.
- To go to the graduation
- To join the neighborhood party

Three reasons why you want a glass of water:

- To take some vitamins
- To gargle
- I need a chaser for a drink.

The justification has to be something you can do.

- I need water for the flowers.
- I need water for an aspirin.

Instant justification will awaken your ability to experience the activity.

EXAMPLE:

Why are you knocking on the table?
You can say:

- To get attention from the actors
- To test its strength

But you cannot say, "I am knocking on the table because I am angry." That is making up something inside yourself; you cannot go to the emotions for your justification. Don't bring in an extra emotional reaction because you don't have it. Rather, you must go to the immediate circumstances, to an activity that is instantly do-able.

EXAMPLE:

Why are you opening the drawer to this dresser?

- To get a pencil
- To take out my keys
- To get stamps for a letter
- To see if the handle of the drawer has been repaired

Each justification must have a logic: You open a drawer in order to get a pencil and some stationery to write a letter. Justification must go on all the time; it is the prime source of awakening you to doing.

You can visualize this if, out of the rehearsal space, we create a garden with trees and a pool. If you are given two or three things to do around the garden and the pool, you must justify each action. Practicing instant justification, you must deal only with the circumstances in front of you.

Action: To spend the afternoon in the garden

"I am going to climb a tree."

This statement, describing an activity without an inner purpose, is not enough in itself. You need to say why you do it. ·

"I'm going to climb a tree to pick an apple."

Now we are given the justification. Actors are often tempted to expand on the reason by saying, "I'm going to climb a tree to pick some apples to give to my friends." The friends have been brought unnecessarily into the scene, and they don't belong there. You can say, "I want to climb the tree to get a nice juicy apple that is good to eat." Now the apple begins to take on the life of the place. To say that you want to give some apples to your friends is simply fake plotting.

Try some other activities in this garden by the pool. Why do you put your hand in the water? Quite simply, to save the butterfly. Just continue in the circumstances, and you will discover what else you can do.

EXAMPLE:

Why did you wipe your hand?

• I want to put on suntan lotion.

Why did you go to the chair?

• Not because you are tired and you want to sit down. That's a lie. Instead, you went to the chair to get a towel.

Why are you reaching down with your right hand?

• Not to get a match, which you don't need.

Instead, reach down for something you need when you lie in the sun, such as sunglasses.

The point is to continue with the logic of being in the particular circumstances of spending the afternoon in the garden.

EXERCISE #34

In order to justify the following questions, what you choose should stimulate you. Why are you

1. Coming out of a building?
2. Going into a store?
3. Walking the dog?
4. Carrying packages?
5. Stopping at the corner?

Use your imagination in the answer. Don't choose words like hot, cold, comfortable, or beautiful because they are not easy to do for an actor. I will physicalize all of these words for you.

COMFORTABLE:	I turned on the air conditioner to be comfortable.
	I took off the blanket to be comfortable.
HOT:	I turned off the radiator because I was hot.
	I opened the window because I was hot.
COLD:	I put on my sweater because I was cold.
	I made a fire because I was cold.
BEAUTIFUL:	I took a picture of the flowers because they were beautiful.
	I bought the vase because it was beautiful.

MORE CREATIVE JUSTIFICATIONS

"Why are you taking the man across the street?"
"Because he is blind and no one else bothered to help."

This is a more creative justification. You will have total belief if your imagination is working. Belief comes from the justification that you choose. Each justification must pass through your imagination so that it becomes more personal and thereby more interesting and vivid to the audience.

EXAMPLE:

- Why are you reading the book?
  The book explains the technique of acting.
- Why are you fixing the chair?
  It's an antique and I can give it to a museum.
- Why are you taking off one shoe?
  I needed to get the circulation going in my toes.

EXAMPLE:

- I'm closing the window because it's blowing napkins off the table.
- I'm closing the door because there's a clattering of dishes going on.
- I'm opening the door because there's no address on it and the guests won't know where to go.

LEFT: Sarah Adler as Katusha Maslova in Leo Tolstoy's *Resurrection* at the Grand Street Theatre in 1903.

RIGHT: Jacob Adler in 1920.

ABOVE: Stella, Sarah, and Luther Adler in Leo Tolstoy's *Kreutzer Sonata* at the Novelty Theatre around 1910. BELOW: Stella Adler in *The Beautiful Lady*, a one-act play performed on the Orpheum Vaudeville Circuit around 1920. RIGHT: Stella and Luther Adler in John Lawson's *Success Story*, performed by the Group Theatre at the Maxine Eliott Theatre in 1932.

RIGHT: Stella Adler as Bessie in *Awake and Sing*, performed by the Group Theatre and directed by Harold Clurman at the Belasco Theatre in 1935. (VANDAMM STUDIO, THE BILLY ROSE THEATRE COLLECTION, NEW YORK PUBLIC LIBRARY)

BELOW: (LEFT TO RIGHT) Morris Lannbusky, John Garfield, Art Smith, Stella Adler, and Phoebe Brand in *Awake and Sing*. (VANDAMM STUDIO, THE BILLY ROSE THEATRE COLLECTION, NEW YORK PUBLIC LIBRARY)

LEFT TO RIGHT: Harold Clur-man, Stella Adler, and Clif-ford Odets looking at the script for *Awake and Sing* in 1936. BELOW: Playbill for *Paradise Lost* by Clifford Odets, performed by the Group Theatre, with Stella Adler playing Clara, in 1936. (PLAYBILL® is a registered trade-mark of Playbill Inc.)

ABOVE: Stella Adler in Hollywood in 1937. (THEATER COLLECTION, MUSEUM OF THE CITY OF NEW YORK) LEFT: Stella Adler and John Payne in the film *Love on Toast,* directed by E. A. Dupont in 1937. BELOW: Stella Adler and Harold Clurman at the opening of the Harold Clurman Theatre in 1979. (ALICE CHEBBA WALSH)

Stella Adler acting for one of her classes in 1976.
(© RUE FARIS DREW)

Stella Adler in 1980. (IRENE GILBERT)

LEFT: Stella Adler teaching one of her classes in 1985. (JIM NETTLETON) BELOW: Stella Adler receiving a Doctor of Fine Arts degree from Smith College in 1987. (MICHAEL ZIDE)

Choose justifications to which you immediately react. For you must really believe in what you are saying. Through justification you have a real place in the theatre because you are giving life to the lines. This contribution is called the actor's "histrionic truth." If you do not use your imagination, you have made no contribution to the play.

Justification must have a level:

LIGHT: I won the lottery

MEDIUM: The cold is not catching. I'm delighted. I've thrown out all the medicine. Everybody's healthy, even the baby.

DARK: occurs when you describe a scene in winter on the Bowery or an avalanche in the Alps. One can agitate the menace of those circumstances by adding detail to them. Of the avalanche one can say:

- One has to warm the bodies with towels and blankets.
- One has to get rid of the broken trees and brush to make a path to the hospital.

The addition of agitating details affects the emotions of the actor. The levels go with the circumstances. The doing of actions, backed up by instant justification, relieves the actor of the unreasonable pressure to act by resorting to amorphous and unreliable feelings. People don't act. They experience something. They experience one moment, then the next moment, then the next moment. If the justification is your talent, don't go where your talent can't possibly travel.

Shift the scene so that the stage is a dressing room in a theatre.

- You sit down at the edge of the stage.
  Why do you sit down?

An actor says, "I sit down because I want to get a better perspective of the stage." But I advise him to cut out that phony college word *perspective* and say instead, quite simply, "I am sitting down because I want to see the stage." When you say "I want to get a better perspective of the stage," you have not used words that enliven you. Avoid words that don't warm you. When you see something, you must make me see it too. I won't be able to see it if your choice of words is cold and remote.

When I asked for five reasons why one might complain about going out in the morning, an actor replied:

> "The elevator takes fifteen minutes to get down from the seventh floor. That is the justification for why I hate to take it."

In this justification, which is strong and correct, there is also a danger. The moment you use the first person singular or words like *love* and *hate,* which have high emotional content, the justification demands are stronger. You have to experience the justification when using the "I."

JUSTIFICATION IN THE CIRCUMSTANCES

Use the circumstances and physicalize the props, if possible.

EXAMPLE:

• I helped an old crippled man carry his valise across the street.
JUSTIFICATION:
Traffic was busy.

• Why did the cab driver hold the door open?
JUSTIFICATION:
To help the mother put the children in the cab

The imagination should give you images to which you react.

EXAMPLE:

• Why are you putting the pamphlets on the chairs?
JUSTIFICATION:
Because the lecture is starting

• Why are you locking the door?
JUSTIFICATION:
To test the alarm system

   All these will have circumstances.

• On the street late at night. You ran into the store to call the police.
JUSTIFICATION:
You were robbed.

• In the corridor. You rang all the bells.
JUSTIFICATION:
There was a fire alarm.

   "Get out. Get out. The house is on fire." You rang the bells to get the people out—you physicalized the justification before saying the dialogue.

• In the doctor's office. You turn off the lights.
JUSTIFICATION:
You are studying the X rays.

   Unless the justification awakens you to the situation, the justification will be weak. Keep trying to find other justifications that awaken you.

EXERCISE #35

Give ten reasons why:

1. The man is crossing the street (as you are looking out the window).
2. You close the curtains (in different circumstances).
3. You are helping Mary (in different circumstances).

INNER JUSTIFICATION

Inner justification is what the actor contributes to the lines of the playwright. The author gives you the lines. He does not give you the justification behind them. That is the actor's contribution.

EXAMPLE:

- **CIRCUMSTANCES:** Hospital corridor
  DOCTOR: "Did you give him the medicine?"
  NURSE: "No."
  INNER JUSTIFICATION: The patient stopped breathing.
- **CIRCUMSTANCES:** A restaurant
  HE: "Wouldn't you like some sugar?"
  SHE: "No, thank you."
  INNER JUSTIFICATION: I have diabetes.

The inner justification lies behind the words.

EXAMPLE:

- **CIRCUMSTANCES:** At home
  She helps the man with his coat.
  INNER JUSTIFICATION: He is her husband.
  He helps the young lady with her coat.
  INNER JUSTIFICATION: She's a guest.

This gives you the justification and attitude toward your partner. There is no text.

EXAMPLE:

HE: "Do you think of yourself as being very modern?"
SHE: "No, I don't at all."
INNER JUSTIFICATION: "I'm traditional."

She is traditional and is influenced by another period.

EXAMPLE:

- **CIRCUMSTANCES:** In courtroom
  HE: "Did you agree with the verdict?"
  SHE: "No, I didn't."
  INNER JUSTIFICATION: "He went further than the call of duty."
- **CIRCUMSTANCES:** Restaurant
  HE: "Won't you have another drink?"
  SHE: "No."
  INNER JUSTIFICATION: He always pushes the girl to drink more and more.

ANSWERING FACTUALLY

Answering factually will make you a boring actor. You cannot make a contribution to the words by simply relating facts, adding nothing to them. Justification turns facts into experiences.

EXAMPLE:

HE: "Will you have a cigarette?"
Answer with a strong justification:
SHE: "No, certainly not!"
INNER JUSTIFICATION:
She believes that smoking will poison the atmosphere and kill young children.

EXERCISE #36

Create three short imaginary stories, two or three minutes in length, of something you saw happen. These stories must contain sequences, have growth, epic ideas, and must be graphic and justified. Build the justification as you need it.

CHAPTER SEVEN

Working on the Stage

PROPS

An actor must use his imagination when he works with props. Very often he has to perform with a minimum of props. It is an annoyance to an actor if he does not have a prop to work with, but sometimes the handicap can be turned into an advantage. One has to know what the life of a prop is before he uses it. A gun has its own life. The knowledge of how to use it must be learned by you from places that deal with guns. This is also true of the sword. You must learn the technique of the sword because it has a tradition. The object is truthful and does not lie. It is the actor that lies.

The actor sometimes has to use a gun. Luther Adler once had to pick up a gun and shoot a man. But the gun was not on the table. Luther fired with an imaginary gun, and the man fell dead. The audience was convinced that the gun had been fired because of the perfection with which the actor had used the imaginary object.

In Moscow during a performance at Meyerhold's theatre, there was a bare stage with a plank where a man could stand on a stepladder. The actor had no pole, no line, no fishhook, but when he lifted his arm, one could see the pole and the twitch of the line as the fish took hold of the hook. He was fishing. It was close to genius. It is a perfect illustration of the principle of using an imaginary prop and creating the circumstances.

As actors, you must understand every prop. In the use of props, try to be specific and clear. If the prop is a newspaper, justify looking for some specific section that you want to read. You must not take too much time doing it. Instead, assign yourself a goal in advance.

Look through the paper for that specific section, turning the pages forward and backward until you find it. You know where and when you are going to find it beforehand.

You cannot use a prop unless you give it dignity and unless you have a liking for it. You must work with the prop until you know you can use it.

SMARTENING UP THE ACTION

In life you can be boring. Onstage you cannot afford to be boring, even for one instant. There is a difference between real time and stage time. In life, an action is worth exactly the amount of time it takes to do it. Onstage, thirty years of a person's life must be compressed into two and a half hours.

What you do on the stage needs a certain economy. This is called "smartening up the action," and it is the technique for making real time fit into stage time.

"Smartening up the action" requires preplanning.

EXAMPLE:

If I need to smoke a cigarette:

• The pack should already be opened.
• One or two cigarettes are sticking out.

I cannot be caught onstage fumbling for a cigarette.

EXAMPLE:

If I need to make up:

• I put on lipstick.
• Fix one eyebrow.

This is truthful, but has the element of stage truth. It is "smartened up."

EXAMPLE:

If I write a letter:

• I put a date on the letter.
• Sign it

EXERCISE #37

Do the following activities. Be aware of the amount of time each needs to hold the audiences attention.

    1. Finish a letter.
    2. Set the table.
    3. Get dressed.
    4. Make your bed.

Smarten these actions up.

PERSONALIZATION

Put your own truth into every prop you use, which makes the prop original.

- In reading a magazine, tear out a page.
- In counting your money, throw the change into your pocket.
- In going through your letters, look for a specific one and then throw it away.

    Personalize the props you use by endowing them with some quality that comes from you.

EXAMPLE:

- Personalize the rose you are about to pin on your dress by shaking drops of water off the rose and by taking a thorn off the stem.
- When you put the sweater into the drawer, personalize the sweater by noticing a loose thread and fixing it.
- When you pick up the glass to take a drink of water, notice the lipstick on the rim and wipe it off with a cloth.

EXAMPLE:
    Here are five actors and their action will be: **to take a drink**

ACTOR 1. He takes scotch over the rocks.
ACTOR 2. He takes gin and tonic.
ACTOR 3. He takes straight scotch.
ACTOR 4. She takes a glass of white wine.
ACTOR 5. She takes scotch with water.

This technique will make you realize that the bottles and the props given to you must be made personal through your imagination. The bottles may be all water. You will make them into the drink that you want by personalizing the prop.

The absolute rule is to personalize every prop. Here are more examples:

EXAMPLE: Five actors are taking a cigarette.

ACTOR 1. He opens and smokes a new package of Kents.
ACTOR 2. He takes a cigarette out of a crumpled pack of Pall Malls.
ACTOR 3. He picks up a butt of a cigarette.
ACTOR 4. She smokes a cigarette from a cigarette holder.
ACTOR 5. He takes the cigarette out of the cigarette case.

Each actor must choose a way in which to personalize the stage prop. You must use your imagination, otherwise you have no job on the stage. To merely use the stage manager's prop is false. Every prop and the way it's used must belong to the actor. So personalize all the props you are given to use on the stage.

EXERCISE #38

Added personalizations for the actions, "to take a drink" and "to smoke a cigarette" are:

1. The bottle of scotch may be three-quarters empty.
2. The glass may be dusty.
3. You may add lemon to your drink.
4. You might smoke from any of the three packages on the table.

Find three or four more.

EXERCISE #39

Do the following:

1. When you comb your hair, don't simply run the comb through, but work out the gnarls or curls or pins.
2. When you put on a sweater, untangle the sleeve.
3. When you paint the chair, wipe the seat clean with a cloth.

Stage Manager's Prop	**Actor's Personalization**
a. The lipstick	Wrong color
b. The mirror	Dirty
c. The letter	Where did it come from?
d. The candlestick	Candle is running
e. Salt and pepper	It needs refilling.
f. Book	Turned upside down
g. Ashtray	Chipped
h. The mail	Mixed up
i. Wallet	Torn in the corner

The added detail each time is your personalization of the object. The way in which an actor personalizes his props, can often make a performance memorable. I remember an actress who, when signing her name in prison, spilled some ink and covered it with her hand, or the actress who when begging for money turned around and held out her hand from her back. The talent of an actor is evident in how he chooses, handles, and personalizes each prop.

Practice constantly with props and costumes that are unfamiliar to you. Don't allow props to frighten you. Make them your own.

Truth on the stage is not quite the truth in life. It is always more or less than life. Onstage you never do exactly what you do in life. If I'm going to put on the cape and look for the button, it's going to look very bad. If you are buttoning your cape, there can be no acting. The cape is large, and the tiny detail takes away from it. Buttoning is wrong for the cape.

—Konstantin Stanislavski

When you use props such as:

- A cane
- A lorgnette
- A fan
- A top hat
- Glasses
- Clothes you wear

props must be used truthfully and should be personalized from the point of view of the character.

Everything you do and everything you wear has a certain value, and other values can be added. What else could the man in the high hat or the man in the cape use? He could use a cane. Try holding the cane as he would. Don't be afraid to control it. Swing it right up, and walk. Swing your whole arm. Don't be afraid of it and don't be stiff.

Adjust to the prop. Let a pair of glasses give you the character. Never play the character. One road to characterizing is to do things. The prop helps you to do your action and can give you a key to your character. The hat, the glasses, and whatever you put on or take up affects the interior, the inside, the soul of the actor.

If all of these props are used conventionally, they will have no impact on your character. Work on each thing specifically until the habit becomes your own. Whatever you have worked on must become second nature to you.

Everything must be controlled; an accent or regionalism, a speech defect, or a specific walk all need practice. So each prop has its own nature and culture. Don't bring yourself and your culture onto the stage with the props. Work on them.

EXAMPLE:

The actor who wears the top hat comes from a specific class, he has:

- Controlled speech
- Controlled walk
- Controlled mind

In the society of that hat, the human being and the clothes were in control. It is from the props, costume, and speech that your character starts to develop. Obey the props and the circumstances.

PLANNED ACCIDENTS

In the professional theatre, you have no right to do anything onstage that is not in your control. Unplanned accidents cannot be permitted. An accident has to be arranged beforehand and practiced several times to make sure that each time it will come about in the same way.

• Take your gloves out of your coat and a card falls out.
• A pen rests on my open book. As I pick up the book, the pen falls out of the book and onto the floor, and I must reach down to pick it up.
• I take out a handkerchief from my coat and some money falls out.

Practice each accident several times after you have arranged it, before you do it on the stage, to make sure that it will work consistently and in exactly the same way each time.

From the props you can determine the class of a character and the epoch he lives in. Props and costumes create an authority in you that makes the character bigger.

COSTUME

What you wear as well as what you do indicates what period you come from and what social class you belong to. The costume helps you become your class. There is, for example, a class difference between a shawl and a muff, the shawl identifying the working-class woman who doesn't care about herself or her appearance, the muff signifying the elegance of the upper-class lady.

In past eras, the costume was of utmost importance, since it created distance between one class and another. It gave you a sense of who you were.

The action and the costume go together. In order to have actors understand this, I had them get down on the floor and dig potatoes—to lie down in the earth, to scratch themselves, to spread their legs, to roll over, without shame. The working class is a physical, touching class, close to the earth, and without romanticism. I got the actors to do a peasant dance, bump into one another, and sing. Then I asked them if they felt closer to their costumes now, and they agreed they did.

In the works of Charles Dickens and the Irish playwrights, you will encounter the working class. You will also get that class in plays written after the 1930s. The costume is immediately revealing of the class and gives the actor an immediate inspiration and an unconscious relationship to the character.

To illustrate aristocracy, I ask actors to look at books of fifteenth- and sixteenth-century paintings of aristocrats. Paintings of aristocrats' costumes are of utmost value to the actor. One can also get ideas about makeup—the costume of the face—from these paintings.

Every actor brings his personal body habits onto the stage, but he must avoid these habits because the character doesn't need them. The costume is really the only way that will help the actor to create an inner self of the character.

CHAPTER EIGHT

Character

The first and most important approach for the actor is to read the play and find out what the playwright wants to say to the world. The actor must discover the important ideas that the playwright reveals through his characters. The playwright wants to reach out and state his opinion about society. Although a play may be in a particular locale, it is meant to reach the world through its ideas. This is the goal of Shakespeare, Ibsen, Shaw, and Strindberg, among others.

We will now go into some of the problems of acting in a play.

Acting is largely based on the differences between characters. An Italian designer, a Russian peasant, a Chinese diplomat all behave in specific ways. They hold themselves differently, walk, talk, think, smoke cigarettes, and laugh differently. Their backgrounds, education, physical manner, moralities, and conditioning are wholly dissimilar.

The actors must not only create these national and occupational traits, but he must also show the differences between characters. Acting is human behavior assembled in novel and interesting ways. Even an archetypical figure like Hamlet can be portrayed by many new character interpretations.

Preparation of your character naturally begins with the playwright's text.

The circumstances that the playwright gives you will make you aware of such important elements as:

- Social situation
- Class
    - Working class
    - Upper-Middle Class
    - Middle class
    - Aristocracy

- Character's profession
- Past of the character
- Character elements
- Character's attitude toward his partner.

These allow you to increase your character's size—you cannot play Hamlet without understanding what it is to be a prince—and to react to the circumstances around him.

SOCIAL SITUATION

Social situation includes:

- Religion   • Morality
- Education   • Money
- Family life   • Sex
- Ethics   • Political situation

Every playwright—Eugene O'Neill, Arthur Miller, William Inge, Anton Chekhov—writes in his own time. If a playwright of the 1970s wants to write about the 1950s or 1940s, he will have to research the period. The actor has the same problem.

In your own time, you must know these things about the past if you go back in history. When you work on a part, it is important to think through how a character lives in his social situation. One should not attempt to perform in a play such as *Waiting for Lefty* without making a thorough study of the 1930s. An actor should read the literature of the time to become familiar with the position of labor and of unions. In the same way we would have to study the 1960s and the 1970s to understand the changing status of blacks in American society. In rehearsing any Shaw play, one cannot escape coming to terms with the strong interest all his characters have in who runs the government, who controls the church, where the power lies.

One could not play *A Streetcar Named Desire* or *The House of Connolly,* Paul Green's 1931 play about the decadence of the Southern aristocracy, without knowing the cultural and social position of the South in American history, without knowing, for instance, that in Southern family life there is a fear of mixed blood.

CLASS

It is important for the actor to know the difference between his own class and the class of his character.

The Aristocracy

The aristocratic man inherits a strong physique and is in exuberant health. This health implies war, adventure, and everything that embraces strong, free, and cheerful actions. These aristocrats were happy, favored by God. Goodness, strength, and nobility were the aristocratic virtues. The basic idea of the well-born aristocrat is to live a good, happy, and beautiful life. The nobility described the lower classes with pity and indulgence. This was handed down from old aristocratic values that the lower classes had to accept. The aristocrat lives with confidence and openness. In the face of the enemy or of danger, the aristocratic spirit displays enthusiasm, gratitude, or revenge. The leveling down of the European man is our greatest danger. This is what depresses us. Today we see nothing that wants to become greater, and we suspect that all goes forever downward, becoming thinner, cozier, more indifferent, more anything. Herein lies the crisis. With the fear of Man we have also lost the love of Man, the reverence for him, or the hope in him. The prospect wearies us—we are tired of Man.

The Upper-Middle Class

The upper-middle class is a monied class and has great wealth, but it has earned it, not inherited it. What this class did inherit from the aristocracy was the wealth of being educated, the understanding of the values of architecture, of literature, philosophy, history, music, and art. When you see an upper-middle class man, you notice that he has a certain manner. This manner enables him to talk to a king or queen, although he did not inherit this tendency. He is a man of distinction, taste, and size. He saved America once by lending the banks a hundred million dollars. As a type, the upper-middle class is shrewd, intelligent, and powerful. Money and power go together: Money, mind, and power can go together. The artist and the wealthy upper-middle class understood that they could live in history by creating symbols of themselves. Lasting symbols, like J. P. Morgan when he created the Frick Museum, and Guggenheim, the Guggenheim Museum, and Rockefeller, the Rockefeller Institute. Man creates the symbol by creating the culture of the country.

This class could be called the aristocrat of the mind.

The Middle Class

We go now from that cultivated class to the real middle class, without the aristocratic mind. We are leaving the class of deep elegance of mind and are going to the practicality and ambition of the middle class. Middle-class thinking and behavior were infected by an emphasis on money, not on culture. Shaw said, "Aristocracy was materialized, the Middle Class was vulgarized, the Lower Class was brutalized." So we get a class of people who think conventionally. The vulgarity of conventional thinking has crept into that person, who then believes it is the truth. So we get a class of people who are practical and ambitious. People who believe what somebody told them. The middle class arose from industrialization, when many people sought to produce things that made money. The technical world arrived. The world was swept up by the ability to produce and a new class of people were stimulated to join this movement.

The middle-class man is neither sincere nor honest nor straightforward—he could have money. His mind loves hiding places; everything hidden impresses him, as his world is security and comfort. He knows self-deprecation and self-humiliation. A race of such men in the end will, of necessity, be more clever than the aristocratic race. Cunning, to a much greater degree, is a vital condition of his survival. This particular class had to be a success. It had to have some kind of success value in it. That aim reduced everything. The interest in individual growth and the inherited values of art declined. The age of industrialism and capitalism swept through the minds and hearts and souls of the people, but to achieve this they gave up the other side of themselves. The climate of the whole country was affected by the capitalist point of view. Capitalism was a great force and has slowly helped to lessen people's respect for themselves, respect for education, respect for art and language, and their respect for each other. Now we are without any tradition at all. From all this comes the rundown quality of man.

The Working Class

The working class in America has gone through many phases, and one experiencing it cannot understand it.

There is no way to talk about the contemporary working class. In America it no longer exists in its purest form. So we will have to go back in history for the spirit of the working class before trade unionism made it into a business.

The working class derives from the European peasant class, small farm workers from the country, before we had modern cities and high-rise buildings. They were a class that went right back to the land. So the place was the land and the land became a city. The workers' needs were simple; they built log cabins with their hands, planted, and ate from the land. Men and women didn't grow old as they do now, their work preserved them. They didn't have arthritis. They worked together; they sang, danced, drank, and had fun together.

This class is built upon the basic principle of working from the land. It is impossible to think of this historical working community without thinking of their games and music. Working-class people always played an instrument, the harmonica, or the guitar, and as time went on they adapted themselves to other instruments, other games. The workingman comes from a community of earth and work. The workingman had a sense of self, a sense of power. He respected himself and said, "I'll work till I die!" He was a man, nothing bent, nothing crooked, nothing broken. He moved very freely, very deliberately. He was not a slob or a bum. He lived on his land in his log house with a fence around him. He lived the way a man could live, the best way he could in his circumstances. Whether he had heavy machinery or a wooden plow to mend, he would deal with it. He would do his job. An honest man's work. You can't call the workingman in America today the working-class man. It is a tradition and it was handed down from father to son. It is different now.

Class distinctions were absolutely without compromise in other periods. In our own time there are no social aspirations. We have democratized all the classes.

PLAYING A PROFESSION

To begin to get used to the extraordinary variety of roles an actor may be called upon to play, ranging from the tyrant on the throne to a petty shopkeeper, the actor needs to practice playing professions of all kinds:

Tailor	Florist	Doctor
Dentist	Baker	Policeman
Bank teller	Archaeologist	Hairdresser
Nurse	Prostitute	Nun

The list is virtually endless. In studying a character, one of the first questions to be asked is: What is his or her profession?

This must be settled before an action can be performed.

For the actor, the study of professions has a number of side benefits. You must go out into the world to study the character and the characteristics of the professional.

EXERCISE #40

Let's start with the hairdresser, taken as a sample in your own time:

1. What are the actions that he does?
2. What is the costume?
3. What are the props befitting the job?

Bring the profession to your own home and do as much of the profession as possible. Practice the actions of the character that you have observed. Use the props necessary. The profession should affect some change in your personality.

Keep working physically with your props. Do some activities where you have to use the props such as:

1. Cleaning hairbrushes
2. Getting a tint ready
3. Arranging curlers

Now add three more professions:

1. A tailor
2. A florist
3. A nurse

Costume is of ultimate necessity in revealing a character's profession. You must always use the costume. Don't indicate the profession. Choose what you will wear down to your shoes and socks, even your underwear. This will make clear what class you are playing and also give you confidence.

BACKGROUND OF THE CHARACTER

The background is created out of the five W's:

"Who" are you?	I am an actor.
"What" is your action?	To act
"When" is this happening?	In the winter of 1987
"Where" is this happening?	In a Broadway theatre
"Why" are you there?	I have an interview.

When these "W" questions are answered, the background falls into place. Without background there is no character. Let's give you the background of daffodils. Consider the daffodils' history or background:

The background of the daffodils:
The daffodil is now your character:

• Born in a nursery in Holland, they were transplanted to grow in special soil.
• They were sent to the flower market in Amsterdam.
• They were bought at the flower auction.
• They left in a plane as air freight.
• From Kennedy Airport, they were sent to the florist in the village.

We now know the background of the daffodils.
You must know similar background detail about the character you play. The background should lead you to your character. Before you can live convincingly in the present on the stage, you must have a fully realized past. You must imagine in detail the early life, family history, educational training, professional experi-

ence, and personal relationships of the character you are playing. The first thing an actor should do when preparing a character is to give his character this sort of background or history.

EXAMPLE: Past of the Character Who Is a Shop Manager

An actor's action was to manage a shop. The character was middle-class. He was dressed formally because the shop was built on the tradition of the old world.

- He was very efficient, since he was brought up in Europe.
- He knew the value of every item.
- He was a serious man, which means, in acting terms, he could lecture on the antiques in his store. For one cannot play "serious." The actor must find an action which will convey his character as being very serious.
- He would go home and discuss various articles with his father, who was also an antique dealer.

This gives you some of the circumstances to help create the profession of managing the store. From this, you can write pages on the shop manager's past.

Additional Background for Shop Manager:

His family lived among things of the old world.

His father realized when, as a child, the boy became interested in antiques, that he should be instructed in languages.

When he came home from school he would always look forward to playing games with his father with the new words he had learned. His father would have him put all his new words into sentences.

He was very mischievous. He would tease his father, telling him that he wanted to be a cowboy when he grew up.

Every day, he would read aloud with his father before dinner. Dinner was very formal. He had to change clothes to sit at the table. He and his mother would talk at dinnertime. His mother was very interested in what he had accomplished so they told her, during dinner, what he had learned that day. She would be so proud of him that she would give him presents—extra chocolate or a new set of pencils. She was delighted when, as he grew up, he would explain to her the different styles of crystal and would teach her the difference in the patterns of silver. She started to become a scholar. Both the boy's father and the boy enjoyed watching this happen to her. He was proud of his mother. She would talk to a customer about the value of crystal, and when she would make a big sale—because crystal was very antique and very special—they would go to a nice restaurant for dinner.

When he was eighteen, he had his first taste of wine. They decided then that there ought to be wine at the table at home when they had dinner.

He became meticulous about what he knew. He would read and mostly do research—both at school and at home. He understood he would really be able to work if he looked like a European sales manager.

His clothes were English in style. He fussed over how his shirts were pressed and his shoes were polished.

He was cheerful and good-natured. When customers would have no idea what they wanted to buy, he would help them make their decisions.

We meet him at twenty-one, when he is able to be called upon by the other shop managers for his knowledge of crystal and silver.

EXERCISE #41

---

1. Draw the circumstances of the shop on a piece of paper so you know how to lay out the acting space. Put the space in your mind and use it when rehearsing in your own room.
2. Walk around in the circumstances of the shop, which has in it:

    a. Shelves with objects
    b. A table with antiques
    c. Another table to write orders
    d. Two chairs

Study the life behavior of the profession. Observe the actions of the shop manager away from the circumstances of his job. For example:

- At home
- Among intimate friends
- Socially

Is he good-natured, sloppy, organized? These are character elements. For this particular character, he is happy, organized, humorous, efficient.

CHARACTER ELEMENTS

- Carefree
- Outgoing
- Responsible
- Adventurous
- Reliable
- Introspective

- Ambitious
- Enterprising
- Conscientious
- Scholarly
- Practical

You find the character element in the world. You watch it and then you can take that element and put it into circumstances that are true for you. Therefore, you can draw upon the world for deep knowledge of the character elements.

By taking the character elements from life, you can develop qualities in your acting you don't ordinarily call upon.

Ways to find character elements:

1. Go to the world and observe
   a. Animals
   b. Objects
   c. People
2. Go to your imagination.
3. How would you physicalize the character elements you have observed?

EXAMPLE: Carefree
Let's start with the character of a bird.

- He lands anywhere
  1. Limb of a high tree
  2. Chimney
  3. Lamppost
  4. Bush
  5. Rock

The bird is living in his circumstances.
The character element is carefree.
The character element can now be used by the actor as follows:

EXAMPLE: A carefree boy

- He jumps on a bike.
- He slides down the banister.
- He swings around a lamppost.
- He leaps over the fire hydrant.

You now have his character. The character doesn't think twice about using his circumstances and his character element is "carefree."

Put him in different circumstances. What would he do?

- He does something suddenly and unexpectedly.
- He jumps into the pool unclothed.
- He comes in jogging clothes to a formal party.
- He goes into the kitchen when invited to a party.
- He jumps onto a bus.
- He throws his arms around friends.

He is animated, lively, and is in continuous movement. Carefree also has:

- Lack of logic
- No responsibility of outside world
- Unfixed in life
- Rhythm of aimlessness

If you are cast in a role in which **reliability** is the chief characteristic:

- Observe reliability in life.
- Imagine a situation where the circumstances demand your reliability.
- Ask yourself in what situation you would be absolutely reliable.

Having found this character element, what do you do in the circumstances you found it so that you will not be so general? What physical activity do you do to show reliability?

EXAMPLE: Meticulous:

- The doctor, in an exam, was meticulous.
- When he washed his hands, he was meticulous.
- When he wrote out the prescription, he was meticulous.

I can now use this character element in acting a part.

- My character is meticulous when he serves the food.
- He is meticulously clean when getting his clothes together.
- He is meticulous when he gives me the telephone messages.

I myself am extremely careless about everything, but I can say that I am meticulously careful in my stage life. Nothing is where it shouldn't be. Therefore, in playing a part, I can draw upon the deep knowledge of the character element of meticulous. By expanding certain personal elements, you can develop qualities that you don't ordinarily call upon. You will be required to play:

- A killer
- A crook
- A liar
- A genius
- A god

and other characters. Begin immediately by spying everywhere for the character elements: They may not always be within your experience.

ATTITUDE TOWARD YOUR PARTNER

Onstage, you must always have a reason to speak. The reason must come from:

- The circumstances
- Your partner
- The text of the play

Everything comes from the justified circumstances.
Every actor, as in life, creates an attitude toward the people or things that surround him.
Toward:

- Ice cream
- The Bible
- Garbage cans
- God
- Your bank manager
- Your mother
- Cigarette smoking
- Spicy food

We all have attitudes toward life:

- Nuns toward drunks
- Man toward his dog
- Dog toward a stranger
- Girls toward a present

The list goes on and on and on.

From your character's point of view, you will get an attitude toward your partner.

As soon as you know your character, your character will give you attitudes, not your personal attitude, but your character's attitude.

This is the way to get an attitude toward your partner. You must know your partner's actions. Whether you are alone or with a partner or partners, the situation you are in needs justification and background. You must build enough of a relationship with your partner so that you have a clear idea of who he is. This will help you in your character.

In all cases, the partner is needed to give you your action, and you have to know the partner's attitude toward everything. Dialogue exists not on cue but when you understand and react to your partner. You must know your partner's part as well as your own.

Your action and your partner's action must be alive enough to get you started. The partner need not always be another actor; it can be an object or a place.

The place itself can stimulate the action.

One can have an attitude toward:

- A room
  a. In the room you write a letter.
  b. Fix the window
  c. Read a magazine

- A forest
  a. In a forest you pick up a stick.
  b. Fix your gun
  c. Use your camera

  Whatever feeds you is a partner.

EXERCISE #42

You develop an attitude toward people because of what they look like and what they do.

Recall attitudes you developed toward people you've seen in your daily life.

1. A dog on the street
2. An aggressive person on the subway

Collect twenty different attitudes from observed conditions in the street. Write them down.

Everything you choose, passing through your imagination must add to character.

In the play you are given words that make sentences, which lead you to plot and circumstances. Every present leads you to the past and clarifies what you are doing.

DIALOGUE

Here is your first play with dialogue. In a script the actor should indicate, as below, his actions/moods/activities/steps on the page opposite from the dialogue.

THE OVERALL ACTION OF THIS PLAY: The laws of humanity and family life are changing in this world.

Diagram

Action	Mood	Activities	Steps
	Medicinal (everyday general mood of the hospital)		
To visit the patient		Arthur looks at clipboard, takes her pulse	To chat about the woman
		John picks up newspaper	
		John picks up medical journal	
To discuss family life		Arthur picks up baby book leafs through it	To discuss family life

Know the social situation for both doctors:

• • • • • • • •

Religion Education Family Life Ethics Morality Money Sex Political Situation

Play with Dialogue

Characters:

Dr. Arthur Armstrong, 45, on the hospital medical board

Dr. John Hilton, 27, assistant

Plot: A woman is contemplating having a baby. She already has two children. The doctors are discussing the situation.

Circumstances: New York Hospital, New York City, New York, 1987.

The scene opens in a hospital room. DR. JOHN HILTON is in the hospital room leafing through a baby book. DR. ARTHUR ARMSTRONG enters the room.

ARTHUR: Good morning, John. (Moves across the room to the bed.)

JOHN: I went over the charts. She's in very good condition.

ARTHUR: Yes, I see. (JOHN moves to the window.) I'm very glad for her. She's extremely anxious because she does want children but she works and her two children are in foster homes.

JOHN: If I were her doctor (moves to bureau), I would recommend that she give up Dr. Spock and realize her ideas are old-fashioned.

ARTHUR: (Sits in chair by the bed.) There is something I want to talk to you about. (JOHN sits by bureau.) What family life are you talking about? You know children have an unhealthy attitude toward their parents and religion. They have nothing to hang on to.

JOHN: Well, my own opinion is that in the working class there is a shortage of money and the woman has to work. This means that family life has suffered because of economics. This shatters everybody.

ARTHUR: I know that your main interest is in research, so you have to give me the privilege of caring for people and their feelings about family life.

JOHN: She's all yours. (He leaves.)

The actors are responsible for familiarizing themselves with the circumstances of the two characters.

ATTITUDE

Dr. Armstrong to Dr. Hilton: Arthur Armstrong is patient and understanding of John Hilton. He wants to teach this younger doctor. He feels that freedom and dishonesty have depraved sex and family life.

Dr. Hilton to Dr. Armstrong: John Hilton respects Arthur Armstrong, but is agitated by the thinking of the older doctor. He wants to get him to change his old-fashioned ideas.

Each doctor wants to clarify what the other's patterns of thought are.

BUILDING A PLOT

Every play has a plot. The dialogue will make you understand the plot, and the characters will reveal themselves through the plot. Every character has a background upon which the character is developed. All this and other elements create the play which contains all of the above elements and more.

Every plot has to grow into new acts or new scenes. A plot and the way it grows must be very clear to the actor who is playing a specific character.

BACKGROUND

DR. ARTHUR ARMSTRONG

Arthur Armstrong comes from an old family background—several generations of Americans. He was brought up in a traditional and old-fashioned home and strongly believes in the family. He had a good relationship with his father. His family influenced him in his manner and he is extremely well equipped for his profession. He was educated in a private school system and his higher education was in England.

Dr. Armstrong's family was conservative and Roman Catholic. He believes that family is important and that you should have children. There were three children in his family and he was the only son. He believes the role of the woman is to be a mother. He thinks that the politics of today are for today only and that they will pass.

He is a medical specialist and is on the medical board at the hospital. He has written books, lectures often, and he is well off financially.

Arthur Armstrong does not believe in abortion. He feels that it is the woman's privilege to have children.

DR. JOHN HILTON

John Hilton loved science as a child. When his family noticed his interest, they began to take him to zoos and museums. They were very supportive of him and he would study things that awakened him. He was allowed freedom. He did not have to live under "do as I do" or "do as I say." He went to Harvard Medical School, where he studied medicine so that he could do research.

Dr. Hilton's family was liberal and Protestant, but not very religious. He feels that family life is going amok and changing greatly under present conditions. He does not believe you should marry on the basis of sexual attraction. He believes that you should live a free life and be able to create a family if you can afford it.

He sees politics as depraved and feels that the government is interfering with the livelihood of doctors today.

He is interested in the growth of his profession and is neutral to money.

John Hilton believes in abortion.

Know your partner's action and be able to take over if you have to play that part. An actor can play the opposite part. He must do the same work that he does when preparing his own part.

LEVELS

In the play, the author gives you certain levels to work on:

• Light
• Dark
• Medium

The actor can be drawn to only one of these levels.

• If the play is on a light level it is a comedy.
• If the play is on a dark level it is a drama.

Take the plays:

• *Hamlet*
• *Macbeth*
• *The Master Builder*
• *Mrs. Warren's Profession*

These are all on a dark level. Most of the plays that end tragically are on a dark level.

The plays of:

- Noel Coward
- Neil Simon
- Oscar Wilde

are all on a light level.

EXAMPLE OF A PLOT:

In the living room, a husband makes it clear he is leaving. Before he goes he puts on his coat, takes off his ring and leaves it on the table. He goes out and closes the door behind him. Now you know he has gone forever.

The wife picks up the ring, puts out the lights, draws the blinds, and exits in the dark.

We now know the plot. It is dark, the mood is heavy. The plot says that marriage can be broken in this period of life by a man deserting a woman.

We now know the **overall action is: Marriage is no longer binding.**

To realize the action of this story, you must do certain things. Everything that is done, on whatever level, has to serve the plot of the play. One has to know how to work physically with three or four things in a room that will cause you to respond to the situation called for by the imaginative plot of the play.

She:

1. Goes to the crib to take a last look at the child
2. Goes to the table
3. Puts her name on a letter that she has written explaining her situation
4. Goes to take her coat and hat
5. Leaves

Every plot has an action. The action is to leave the house. There are no steps in the action.

EXERCISE #43

Build a Plot and Justify

In the circumstances of this plot:
   He:

1. Entered a room, which was dark
2. Went to the crib and found it empty
3. Opened the window to see if anybody was about
4. Then ran down the stairs to call the police

The use of the "he" enables you to see the circumstances. The next step is to agitate the circumstances by taking it out of the third person and putting it into the first person.

1. I came into the room, which was dark.
2. I listened and heard nothing.
3. I went over to the crib to pick up the baby and the baby was gone.

How much more do you feel when the action is in the first person?

EXERCISE #44

Write ten pages about Mary ("Mary had a little lamb"), saying:

1. Where she went to school
2. Who her brothers and sisters were, or if she was alone in the family, why her parents were not with her

Justify all your statements. Build up the background on a dark level. For instance, the lamb's feet were bleeding, the lamb cried, and Mary cleaned its feet. Now you can say the line, "And everywhere that Mary went, the lamb was sure to go." The present exists because the past is true; one feels the suffering of the lamb and the concern of Mary. The expansion of the story through the creation of the imaginative background makes you feel more.

When you build a background, you must choose things that affect you, aggravate you.

Studying the background will help you guard against the common fault in American acting of bringing yourself onstage without change—you must:

- Change your hair
- Make up your face
- Change the costume
- Change the behavior

Do these things according to the character.

You must know the difference between the play you are playing and your own life—between the person you are portraying and yourself. Hamlet, as we have said, is not a person such as yourself; he owns Denmark. You cannot play Hamlet without working on class differences. The possible overall action that Hamlet takes—to search for his truth in his time—requires a lot of background.

The actor must depend upon the mass knowledge that Man has within him to help him relate to the experience of the character he plays. By working through the background, expressed in actions, not words, he can begin to pull the life of foreign and often forbidding characters such as Hamlet or Lear into himself.

EXERCISE #45

Take a period in history, develop it by researching the music, the literature, the religion, the painters, the architecture, the clothes the people wore, the attitude toward money, and write three or four pages about it.

EXAMPLE:

Year	Politics	Theatre	Visual Arts	Music	Science	Daily Life	Religion
1906							

There is a book that will help you in researching all periods. It is called *Timetables of History* by Bernard Gruen.

CHAPTER NINE

The Vocabulary of Action

What the actor is called upon to do on the stage is as broad as life itself, and the range of actions he should have at his command must be very wide. An actor must begin to acquire a vocabulary of actions, such as:

- To reminisce
- To talk
- To chat
- To converse
- To discuss
- To argue
- To fight
- To take care of
- To explain
- To teach
- To reveal
- To denounce
- To defy
- To dream
- To philosophize
- To pray
- To advise

These are among the more important and frequently used actions, but there are, of course, many more.

TO REMINISCE

The human being is the only animal who is able to recall the past, something which is dead and only he can bring it back. "To reminisce" is a device playwrights often use to bring the poetry of poetic prose into their scripts. A retreat into a more favorably remembered past, reminiscing is itself a means of poetic escape from the sometimes unbearable realities of the present.

The action "to reminisce" is to soliloquize, to recall the past and bring it back. It is different from remembering, which is automatically associated with daily life. You remember your telephone number and your grocery store list. You remember to answer a letter. In reminiscence, the character brings back what he loves. You can say, "One day I was walking along a river. It was flowing quietly. I sat in the shade. I could see the mountains."

The anatomy of the action "to reminisce" is that the character relives the experience—to see again what you once saw and to remember it fondly.

When you start to reminisce, you lose the present world.

EXAMPLE:

> This table I am sitting at no longer exists for me,
> only the river I walked along on that spring day under
> the cloudless sky when I could see the mountains.

When the character brings back a part of his past life through reminiscence, his words take on a poetic quality. "To reminisce" is to bring back a lost world: Everything becomes important and significant because it has gone away.

If you have left the world by going to memories, you can:

- Lose the present
- Bring a poetic quality onstage
- Give life to what has died but still lives in you
- You must visualize each image.
- Use very little physical movement.
- Use very few gestures.
- If you have left the world by going to memories, you can go in and out of reminiscence when you have a partner.

> It is the author's way of creating poetry through prose.
> The action must be lifted to a high level.

Blanche DuBois reminisces in *A Streetcar Named Desire* by Tennessee Williams:

> He was a boy, just a boy, when I was a very young girl.
> When I was sixteen, I made the discovery—love. All at
> once and much, much too completely. It was like you

suddenly turned a blinding light on something that had always been half in shadow, that's how it struck the world for me.

When rehearsing the action of reminiscing, create the background. Start from your immediate circumstances; then you lose them completely.

You can reminisce about something you care about.

• About a character's lost home
• About a family that has scattered and is gone

Go to the text of John Van Druten's *I Remember Mama.* The circumstances are in the period of 1910 in America.

• Think about the costume.
• Reminisce near the circumstances of the ocean.
• Use the circumstances to stimulate you.

Here is Katrin recalling her family:

It's funny but when I look back, I always see Nels and Christine and myself looking almost as we do today. I guess that's because the people you see all the time stay the same age in your head. Dagmar's different. She was always the baby—so I see her as a baby. Even Mama—it's funny, but I always see Mama as around forty. She couldn't always have been forty.

Wordsworth said, "Poetry is emotion recollected in tranquility." You must not activate the circumstances too much. They must exist in tranquility. (Another source of reminiscence is Thorton Wilder's *Our Town.*)

EXERCISE #46

Create an old-fashioned room in the country in the 1900s with:

1. An old upright piano
2. Music sheets
3. A sewing basket

4. A rocking chair
5. A mother
6. An old album of family pictures

Reminisce about each of the above.

Reminisce from within this life. Take the circumstances of an old garret:

1. Go up the creaky stairs.
2. See the spider webs and the old trunk.
3. Reminisce about the objects in the trunk—the broken old doll, etc.

TO TALK, TO CHAT, TO CONVERSE, TO DISCUSS, TO ARGUE, TO FIGHT

The action can begin with "to talk," continue with "to chat," "to converse," and "to discuss," and end with arguing and fighting.

To Talk

You can talk back and forth with a partner about:

- Fixing the sofa
- Repairing the broken light fixtures
- Painting the dirty walls

In this form of communication there are no cues. The art of Talking is that no one is really listening intently. To talk is to interrupt all the time. In daily life, we talk about serious things that do not mean anything to us—the national economy and international politics. We spend our whole life talking about these subjects without experiencing what we are talking about.

To Chat

Chatting has a different tempo which is suggested in the very name of the action, "to chitchat." You chitchat on a light level. Chitchatting is similar to talking in that one listens and chats at the same time. If a group of three or four are chatting together, everyone should have the same tone. Everyone should be equal and no one should attempt to take over.

To Converse

If you were in an airplane, sitting next to someone you didn't know the action probably would be "to converse." You do not really reach the other person. The situation is not given to a lot of deep talk. Conversation is an action that is associated with the middle and upper classes, and has formality about it. The nature of a conversation is that it is not intimate. I don't know you, and you don't know me. In conversation you listen and you answer.

To Discuss

The first requirement of discussion is that both you and your partner have a genuine interest in the ideas that will be discussed. Discussion is a very modern action. The discussive element is found in most modern plays since Ibsen, and consists of stating two contradictory points of view, neither of which wins. There is no need to win the discussion. You can, therefore, discuss without cutting off your partner. The ideas expressed by the partner will excite you: The exchange will stimulate you. Discussion should take place on a subject that is mutually interesting.

In this action, as in almost no other in the field of communication, there is genuine understanding, and the give-and-take is real and unforced. It is, perhaps, the most important action in modern playwriting because the audience understands both sides of the discussion and becomes the third partner in the play. The members of the audience can leave the theater and make up their minds as to which side of the discussion is according to their beliefs.

EXAMPLE: Topics for discussion:

• Should abortion be legal?
• Should the government support the arts?
• Is marriage a good idea for artists?

To Argue

"To argue" means that the actors have two strong points of view, and they cling to them. The anatomy of the action is to grab pieces of the discussion, but you don't really take it in; you go on with your own side and opinion.

To Fight

"To fight" means that there is no control, and very little listening. You attack in all directions. "To fight" is to go after something with no waiting.

From arguing to fighting is a natural progression, and with fighting we have reached the end of the chain of communicating.

To Take Care Of

EXAMPLE: CIRCUMSTANCES—A Lawn

A baby bird has fallen from the nest; its wing is injured. How would you take care of it?

In your chosen circumstances, you can:

• Spread a cloth underneath the bird—which you get from the house
• Feed the bird some water
• Move the bird to the veranda

These are things you can do in your action "to take care of." You can use all of the circumstances for the bird.

This example makes you understand how to take care of an animal. There are no small stories; only the actor makes them small. One finds out that the bird has a life of its own in the action of "taking care of."

In the overall action of this sequence the theme would be that man is helpful to animals and people when there is difficulty.

EXERCISE #48

To take care of a patient in a hospital as a nurse, familiarize yourself with the profession. Live off the circumstances:

1. What is on the medicine table?
2. What is on the report at the foot of the bed?
3. Adjust the air in the room—use the window.
4. Take off the blanket.

This may mean visiting a hospital to observe the care. Practice what you have seen until it becomes second nature to you.

1. Your action of taking care of a patient will stimulate a counter-action in the patient.
2. In these circumstances, you must create a background for your partner.
3. As actors, we must look for the human relationship.
   a. What is your attitude toward the patient?
   b. What is her attitude to you?
   c. Is the action on a dark or light level?

Draw a picture of the room in the hospital. Always draw your circumstances.

To do the action of taking care of someone, you have to justify it so that you are genuinely caring of the patient. The ingredient of caring is your talent. Many actors leave that out completely.

To Explain

"To explain" is to clarify to your partner something that he very much needs to know. It is factual and down-to-earth.

EXAMPLE:

• Explain how to use the air conditioner in your house.

   Know your circumstances.

• Explain why the social situation is difficult in the modern world.
• The abortion problem
• The poor education in public schools

To Teach

The anatomy of teaching is to give in depth what you know about a certain subject to someone who needs to know. Everybody knows how to teach something.

EXERCISE #49

Use teaching in different circumstances through your imagination, show:

1. How to cut a diamond
2. How to shoot a machine gun
3. How to run a chemical lab
4. How to run an office

In order to teach you something I must know something, although, as an actor, it may be far from my experience, such as how to use a machine gun or cut a diamond. If these actions are not known to you, you must put the teaching of them through your imagination.

Choose the circumstances for each of the above actions. Pick three things you do in those specific circumstances.

EXERCISE #50

Practice teaching:

1. How to design a dress
2. How to fly a plane
3. How to drive a chariot

Everybody knows something and what you know you can teach:

4. Horseback riding
5. Quiltmaking
6. Tennis

You can also, through your imagination:

7. Be a woodcutter
8. Make penicillin

To Reveal

A more complex action is "to reveal" oneself. Revealing is opening up the inner self and exposing your deepest thoughts without holding back. It is a universal human experience. Strong feelings are associated with this action, but as in all actions, no attempt should be made to express the feelings. The feelings will come out of the actions.

Every character that you play has very deep experiences. It is the playwright who wrote the characters who reveal themselves.

EXAMPLE:

- One reveals one's illness to a doctor.
- One reveals one's sins in confession.

To reveal is a large and epic action. It does not need a partner. You can express yourself while other people are on the platform doing other things—smoking, drinking quietly, not listening. This public inner revealing of oneself is a very important theatre action in Chekhov's *Three Sisters*. In this play one of the large actions is to reveal the characters' failures in life.

To Denounce

"To denounce" is a strong action that has size. It expresses itself to the enemy. It is close to the action of attack. The action to denounce is:

- To bring your partner down
- To destroy him

It is an action performed by someone with power: from the king to his enemies, or from the strike leader to the bosses, as in *Waiting for Lefty*. Denuniciation goes from one archetype to another. The attack is not on an individual, but on the institution that the individual represents.

To denounce is the action of *Coriolanus* in his "common cry of curs" speech.

You common cry of curs! Whose breath I hate
As reeks of the rotten fens, whose loves I prize
As the dead carcasses of unburied men
That do corrupt my air, I banish you!
And here remain with your uncertainty!
Let every feeble rumor shake your hearts!
Your enemies, with nodding of their plumes,
Fan you into despair!

Or of Dr. Stockmann in Ibsen's, *An Enemy of the People:*

What does the destruction of a community matter if it
lives on lies! It ought to be razed to the ground, I tell
you! All who live by lies ought to be exterminated like
vermin! You will end by infecting the whole country;
you will bring about such a state of things that the
whole country will deserve to be ruined. And if things
come to that pass, I shall say from the bottom of my
heart: Let the whole country perish, let all these people
be exterminated.

The person who denounces believes that nobody can touch
him. It's as if he was a god, not just a civilized man. There is no
pleading in the action, no attempt to remedy the situation.

You need to locate a sense of power in order to denounce,
and it must come from inside you. The action must be in you
before you start. Start by denouncing:

- Bankers
- Oil company operators
- People who start wars

You must find the necessary power and size. A sense of
being somebody, a sense of being somewhere. You must express
the action. You must judge how much energy or effort you need
if you use any gesture.

To Defy

Defiance is close to denunciation. It is another action that
calls for size, for a king, and it is difficult for young actors to

handle. The action of defiance is *to cut down a man, to demolish his ideas.*

In Shaw's *Pygmalion,* when Eliza's moment finally comes, and she defies Henry Higgins, Shaw is saying that there are two classes onstage, and the conflict is that the servant class thinks it is equal to the upper class. That is the overall idea.

Actors have a tendency to become too emotional when speaking defiantly; the words must not get lost in the temperament. Especially in Shaw, the words are the most important thing.

To Dream

"To dream" is to lose the present and is similar to reminiscing. But dreaming differs from reminiscing in that it looks to the future instead of to the past. To dream is to think of something you don't have yet but would like to have. It is to see something before you.

In Robert's monologue in the first act of Eugene O'Neill's *Beyond the Horizon,* the theme is that of the big dream of life, of reaching the sea and experiencing its mysterious force. This excerpt from the monologue is an example of "to dream":

ROBERT

I would start dreaming. I knew the sea was over beyond those hills. . . . There was all the mystery in the world to me then about that—far-off sea—and there still is! It called to me then just as it does now. . . . And I'd promise myself that when I grew up and was strong, I'd follow that road, and it and I would find the sea together.

Robert is struggling to make himself clear. He resists the attachment to reality and longs to return to the sea.

In order to dream, you must leave your body, much as you do in sleep. Your imagination takes control, and you lose the present moment. You are not really concerned with where you are. The dream is strong in images and grows in size, expanding with the imagination. The dream is always visual, and the images must be seen by you. If you see them, the audience will see them.

Excerpt from N. Richard Nash's *The Rainmaker:*

Sister, the last place I brought rain is now called Starbuck—they named it after me! Dry? I tell you, those people didn't have enough damp to blink their eyes! So I get out my big wheel and my rolling drum and my yella hat with the three little feathers on it! I look up at the sky and I say, "Cumulus!" I say: "Cumulo-nimbus! Nimulo-cumulus!" And then I look up and down comes the rain!

To Philosophize

"To philosophize" is to ask what life means, to penetrate the mystery. It's a cool action and is not related to anyone. You can philosophize about death, as in this excerpt from Euripides' *Trojan Women:*

Death, I am sure, is like never being born, but death is better by far than to live a life of pain, since the dead with no perception of evil feel no grief.

And in the Reverend Anthony Anderson's speech from Bernard Shaw's *The Devil's Disciple:*

The worst sin towards our fellow creatures is not to hate them, but to be indifferent to them; that's the essence of inhumanity. After all, my dear, if you watch people carefully, you'll be surprised to find how like hate is to love. . . . Think of how some of our married friends worry one another, tax one another, are jealous of one another, can't bear to let one another out of sight for a day, are more like jailers and slave-owners than lovers. Think of those very same people with their enemies, scrupulous, lofty, self-respecting, determined to be independent of one another, careful of how they speak of one another—pooh! Haven't you often thought that if they only knew it, they were better friends to their enemies than to their own husbands and wives?

To Pray

"To pray" is to reach out for help, for consolation; to beg for help.

EXERCISE #51

Pray to:

1. Zeus
2. God
3. Jesus
4. Buddha

Be aware of praying differently to different images.
Pray to:

1. Get help
2. Give thanks
3. Beg for relief

Always create the circumstances of where you are when you pray.

To Advise

To give advice to a person means that he or she needs to know something that you can make clear. You advise someone about:

- Real estate
- Finances
- Home life
- Personal life

Where do you go for advice?

- Doctor's office
- Lawyer's office
- Parent's house
- Person next door

The anatomy of "to advise" is to have fluency. The action is all mind. The action doesn't come from the heart, it comes from the head. Advising is therefore not like teaching, which goes from my heart to your heart. When you go to a policeman for advice, he doesn't teach you how to get to the subway, nor does the doctor teach you what medicine to take. They advise you.

Excerpt from William Saroyan's *The Time of Your Life:*

Look, kid, you're not getting any younger. Don't be a sucker. It's none of my business. Only let me tell you one thing—love is for the very young or the very rich.

The author is writing about the problems of class, that of the working-class woman.

In order to advise, you must:

1. Know enough about the person you are giving advice to.
2. Work on the script and become familiar with the plot.
3. Know right away what class the playwright is talking about.
4. Know why the play is important.

EXERCISE #52

Now place the action in circumstances.

Draw an outline of the place, which is a kitchen—have a picture of the set and props in your mind.
a. Table
b. Sink
c. Refrigerator
d. Chairs

You must observe the character before advising him. In the scene Janet's clothes may be scattered about and the coffee cups unwashed. Her costume is in disarray. All this detail contributes to the inner justification of the action "to advise." Next, you must begin to create the background of Janet and her partner.

Your impression of Janet:

• Her eyes are bloodshot.
• She dyes her hair.

- Her clothes are dirty.
- She is slouched over.

Taking any four impressions in order will give you the action to advise.

CHAPTER TEN

The Actor's First Approach to the Author

PARAPHRASING

Reading or speaking comes from the words on the page. The actor's understanding of these words during rehearsal must be clear.

Paraphrasing the text of the play is an essential feature of the actor's technique. Paraphrasing is taking the author's ideas and putting them into the actor's words, and thereby making them belong to the actor. Paraphrasing encourages you to use your mind and your voice and gives you some power that equals the author's power. Simply hearing the sound of your own voice can be useful. First, the audience must believe you before they can believe the author.

This is your first essay and is the actor's first approach to the author. The following is an excerpt from Kahlil Gibran's essay "On Marriage" from *The Prophet:*

> You were born together and together you shall be forevermore.
> You shall be together when the white wings of death scatter your days.
> Ay, you shall be together even in the silent memory of God.
> But let there be spaces in your togetherness,

And let the winds of the heavens dance between you . . .

Give your hearts, but not into each other's keeping.

For only the hand of Life can contain your hearts.

And stand together yet not too near together.

For the pillars of the temple stand apart,

And the oak tree and the cypress grew not in each other's shadow.

EXERCISE #53

---

1. What is your reaction to the ideas in the essay?
2. When marriage is entered into, do you think that it should be automatically forever?
3. Do you agree with Gibran's idea that marriage partners should not interfere with each other's personal freedom?

These ideas ask for your reaction and interpretation.

The author's need is to write the play. The actor's most important need is to interpret the play. Use your own words. The above exercise will make the ideas belong to you. You are then in a partnership with the author.

When paraphrasing, always take the ideas that have some importance. It would be helpful for you to read essays, speeches, and newspaper articles and editorials, drawing ideas from them. For that, you must put the text into your own words at first. Then take out the punctuation. When you understand the text, the punctuation will naturally fall where you need it.

EXERCISE #54

Paraphrase the ideas that you have read and then the idea will become a part of you. It is not enough for you to say the words. You must understand them. The following is an excerpt from Kahlil Gibran; "On Talking," from *The Prophet:*

You talk when you cease to be at peace with your thoughts and when you can no longer dwell in the solitude of your heart you live in your lips and sound is a diversion and a pastime and in much of your talking thinking is half murdered there are those among you who seek the talkative through fear of being alone and there are those who talk and without knowledge or forethought reveal a truth which they themselves do not understand.

(Punctuation has been left out intentionally as part of the exercise.)

EXERCISE #55

Read Aloud

Try the same exercise with a newspaper article or editorial, or Shakespearean speech or poetry.

1. Read it aloud. Think of speaking as singing.
2. Understand what you are reading.
3. Paraphrase it.
4. Speak it out quietly in your own words.
5. Project your voice across the room.

An actor is the person who understands that words carry ideas.

When you study texts written in contemporary language, you should choose essays to paraphrase which bring you closer to the idea. Texts that deal with truths lift the actor to the largeness of the text. Don't bring the script down to an everyday level.

SEQUENCES

Break down the text into sequences that are intelligible to you.

The following are three sequences from Charles Dickens's *A Tale of Two Cities:*

- "Monseigneur, one of the great lords in power at the Court, held his fortnightly reception in his grand hotel in Paris."
- "Monseigneur was in his inner room, his sanctuary of sanctuaries, the Holiest of Holiests to the crowd of worshippers in the suite of rooms without."

• "Monseigneur was about to take his chocolate. Monseigneur could swallow a great many things with ease, but his morning's chocolate could not so much as get into the throat of Monseigneur, without the aid of four strong men."

This is what I mean by "sequences." Look for the sequences in a text and follow them. Each sequence is another thought. See how the idea develops. Take in the sequences and don't study the words. Let one sequence lead you to another. This is the secret of working on a script.

THE PROBLEM OF SIZE

American actors are frightened of size. When the playwright's ideas are universal and epic, the actor withdraws. He is afraid of overdoing it. He pulls the playwright's ideas down to their simplest level, which he calls being real on the stage. The actor must get used to working with texts that have problems which affect everyone, such as friendship, loyalty, and family life.

If you can understand and interpret the author's ideas, you will gain size in your performance.

• Why did the author write the play?
• What does the author want to say?

When playing an epic character, don't be afraid to use your voice. Use all of your energy and give yourself ideas that you would fight for. Enrich your audience.

CHAPTER ELEVEN

Working on the Text

THE DISCUSSIVE ELEMENT IN THE MODERN TEXT

The discussion of ideas is at the center of the modern theatre. In many great plays from Ibsen on, one finds what we call the discussive element. From Shaw and O'Casey to Beckett and Pinter, from O'Neill and Odets to Arthur Miller, Tennessee Williams, and Edward Albee, the discussive element is used.

The modern theatre is a theatre of ideas, a theatre whose purpose it is to make an audience think and learn about the larger questions of life.

If two people simply agree on the stage, there is no play and there is nothing more to say. The modern theatre is based on our ability to consider two points of view. In any dramatic situation, one character may be for an idea under discussion and another may be against it. In Ibsen's *A Doll's House*, when Nora announced that she was going to leave, her husband said, "Your first duty is to your husband and your children." Nora said, "No, I think my first duty is to myself."

The discussive element entered the theatre with Ibsen. The middle class introduced accepted values of morality, manners, and ethics that were part of a defined class society. The middle class has only "picked-up" values. This lack of certitude means that for every question that arises, there are two sides. In the modern theatre there is no one truth.

In discussion, one must recognize the difference between issues of varying weight and importance, and judge between the larger and the smaller issues.

One can take the smaller issue that New York is overcrowded and bring in another larger issue.

- Overcrowding is the nature of city life. Every city in the world is going to have an escalation of population.

One can accept this as positive or hold:

- That it can lead to family breakdown, loss of morality, disease and the disaster of overpopulation

In theatre, the interest comes from having an opinion. When you start a discussion on a topic such as the overpopulation of cities, you must stick to the topic and not wander into other epic ideas. You have no right to go far afield or to be general. In discussion, the mind of each partner is alert. You should cool the emotion.

There must be growth in your discussion. Unless it proceeds step by step, you run the risk of becoming repetitive and boring. You should not start with an announcement, such as "I believe . . ." Instead, you should pick up from what your partner says or from what you believe your partner thinks. Continue the subject that is already in the mind of your partner; don't start a new one.

EXAMPLE: Abortion

Proceeding by steps gives growth and interest to your argument. If you are discussing abortion and speaking against it, you can begin by saying:

- The fetus is the start of life.
- Abortion is wrong because it means the killing of life.
- The remedy is not abortion, but the creation of better foster homes and the improvement of adoptive methods.

Discussion exercises are meant to help the actor to understand the themes of modern playwrights, and to appreciate the opposition of ideas. The writer is articulate because he expresses contrary points of view from the stage.

The discussion is not a monologue. You must keep to the level the discussion requires and not be lower in tone than your partner. In modern life there are, for example, the following themes for discussion:

For or Against:

- The role of the woman
- Abortion
- Capital punishment
- The institution of marriage
- Whether marriage is good for actors

EXERCISE #56

Take one or two of these themes and discuss them with another actor. You should be able to live off your partner and be awakened to the theme of what you are discussing. The words come out of the theme.

The actor should be encouraged to use both points of view by reversing parts.

When there is nothing epic or universal about the discussion, it is too small for the theatre. The playwright deals with big subjects. The actor will be talking about man, about life, about society.

Compared to the idea, the individual personality of the actor is insignificant. You must transcend your own personality and assume the largeness of the subject you are discussing. Abortion is not a pedestrian subject. You must not bring to it a pedestrian mind.

Such a question is large enough to go before the United States Senate and the clergy and the people. It should not be brought down to the level of the street. You should not be argumentative in discussion. You must learn the difference between discussion and argument. In this country, we don't know how to discuss; we only argue. We're like taxi drivers. Our own national temperament is intolerant of listening. If the discussion slides into argument, and if you want to fight, you won't listen, and the discussion is finished. You also mustn't take too long with what you say. Winning the discussion is not the point, but learning is. Give absolute attention to what your partner says.

Largely because modern plays focus on discussion, they are written in prose. They are written the way we speak and they are written, too, in a country that is not very verbal. As you speak the lines of a modern play, don't borrow from another culture. Don't add anything that is theatrical or that appears affected. It makes the play less convincing and even false.

Ideas are what draw us to contemporary theatre. What makes you learn and grow is the discussive element. Since 1875, Ibsen has contributed discussive ideas—such as the role of women in society—to the modern theatre. His ideas are still being discussed. We still talk about the Oedipal complex, which was first explored in ancient Greek drama. The ideas that come from the stage take hold and are enduring.

EXERCISE #57

Discussion

Find a big idea in a play by Shaw and describe in three quarters of a page what he is saying:

1. *Major Barbara*
2. *Pygmalion*
3. *Candida*

THE MONOLOGUE

For the playwright, the monologue is a powerful and distinctive way of communicating directly with the audience. When using the monologue, the playwright is openly addressing the world. As a large poetic action, the monologue contains the core of the idea a playwright means to convey to his audience. Shakespeare's theme in *Richard II* is that countries rise and fall, and civilizations, like Man himself, die. In Richard's words, everything leads to death.

In the following soliloquy from Act III of *Richard II*, Richard is lamenting the victorious return of his rival, the banished Bolingbroke.

Of comfort no man speak:
Let's talk of graves, of worms and epitaphs;
Make dust our paper, and with rainy eyes
Write sorrow on the bosom of the earth;
Let's choose executors and talk of wills:

And yet not so—for what can we bequeath
Save our deposed bodies to the ground?
Our lands, our lives, and all are Bolingbroke's,
And nothing can we call our own but death.

Shakespeare is telling us in this passage what it is like to lose
hope and face death.
Goethe said:

If you lose money, you have lost something. If you
lose love, you have lost much. But if you lose hope,
you have lost everything.

Tennessee Williams wrote about this in *Small Planet:*

When a man looks up at a constellation, shrugs his
shoulders, and says 'So what?', then he knows he is
already dead and in mourning for his life.

Mourning comes with the realization that life is not eternal—
when you discover that things do not go on indefinitely and you
lose the will to make them go on. But an author can also be
obscure. Don't always try to make sense out of the monologue,
as in Tom's curtain soliloquy in *The Glass Menagerie:*

I didn't go to the moon. I went much further—for time
is the longest distance between two places. Not long
after that I was fired for writing a poem on the lid of a
shoe-box. I left St. Louis. I descended the steps of the
fire escape for a last time and followed, from them on,
in my father's footsteps, attempting to find in motion
what was lost in space—

Tennessee Williams, whose writing has the quality of poetry, is vague in the first two lines of the monologue. In his
roundabout way, Williams is saying that Tom is not going to stay
home and allow what happened to Laura happen to him.
Read the following excerpt from *Electra* by Sophocles:

Orestes was driving last, purposely holding his team
back and pinning his faith to the final spurt; and now,

seeing only one rival left in, with an exultant shout to his swift horses he drove hard ahead and the two teams raced neck and neck, now one now the other gaining lead. . . . When the people saw his fall from the chariot, there was a cry of sympathy for the poor lad. . . . They saw him now pinned to the ground, now rolled head over heels, till at last the other drivers got his runaway horses under control and extricated the poor mangled body, so bruised and bloody that not one of his friends could have recognized him.

In the above monologue the action is to tell a story. As an actor you must make us see the arena and feel the tension of the horses tearing to go. The story must be taken from sequence to sequence, not from period to period.

The monologue describes nothing less than the death of the Prince of the world. As an actor, you have to feel the magnitude of this event inside yourself and give it back to the audience.

These two monologues are among the most arresting, and difficult, in dramatic literature. You may begin to deal with the monologue on a much simpler level, as Chekhov did in the last act of *The Cherry Orchard,* a monologue to a bookcase.

Do you know how old this bookcase is? A week ago I pulled out the bottom drawer, and I found some figures burnt in the wood. It was made exactly a hundred years ago. What do you think of that, eh? We ought to celebrate its anniversary. An inanimate object, true, but still—a bookcase!

You may begin by delivering impromptu monologues to different objects:

- To a chair
   a. "Chairs have been with us through the ages. They come in all kinds of sizes and shapes, etc. . . ."
- To a wall
   a. "The walls are thick and sturdy, etc. . . ."
- To a ceiling
   a. "The ceiling keeps the rain out, etc. . . ."

The actor endows these objects with personal qualities. He should feed the chair and the wall as he would a live partner—and give them the life they embody. From there, the actor should do monologues about such objects as a tree or a flower.

Good monologues can be found in Edgar Lee Masters's *Spoon River Anthology*. This book contains an almost unlimited succession of characters of endless variety, each caught in a moment of moral or personal crisis.

Some clues on how to do a monologue:

- Avoid gestures, which often come from having no ease with the language.
- Don't use the ordinary quality of language if it is essentially poetic.
- Avoid using props.
- Choose the area which is true for the circumstances.
- It is not good to move around too much in a monologue; therefore, use a limited space.
- Find the rhythm of the monologue, as the playwright always creates a rhythm.
- Costume can contribute to or detract from the effectiveness of a monologue.

In every monologue one must seek a meaning larger than the facts of the situation suggest. The facts ground it. The temptation is always great to start with the words, but this is a bad habit.

If the actor is provoked to go to the words first, he may lose the theme, putting it on a common level rather than the higher level that is needed.

EXERCISE #58

Find a monologue in *Spoon River Anthology* and paraphrase it. Work on the background.

THE TECHNIQUE OF REHEARSAL

Stanislavski said that you can rehearse a play for six hours or you can rehearse it for six months. One rehearsal is very different in its results from the other, but both may be equally valid. Early in your training you need to understand the rehearsal process. Whether you are doing a simple classroom exercise or rehearsing a full-length play, the principles of rehearsal are the same. A finished delivery is not expected of the actor every time he gets up to work. John Barrymore once was offered a part in a very big play. He was asked to read for his role, and he read that part as haltingly as a first-year drama student: "I . . . love . . . you. I . . . cannot . . . live . . . without you." He did not feel obliged in the least to give a perfect reading.

An actor rehearsing a play is like a pianist warming up by doing scales. A Beethoven sonata cannot be performed faultlessly at once.

Stage 1: Taking in the Meaning

Whether for the exercise or for the play, there are three stages of rehearsal. The concept of the rehearsal process is that the actor should first learn his lines. This is a deadly concept. In practice this comes almost last. The first stage of rehearsal is to study the script without memorization, in order to slowly take in the play's meaning and what the author wants to say about Man and the world.

When you start working on the text, you have to be open to impressions. You are starting from the outside. When I go into a garden center, I see thousands of plants and bulbs. They are all unfamiliar to me, and even the language that is spoken does not sound natural to me. I know only that it is a garden center as I know that the play is a play. Although the words in themselves will not at first make sense, from the words and the rhythm of the lines, you can tell whether the mood of the play is dark or light or in the middle: You can determine if it is a comedy or a drama.

Each play has a style. Recognize it as you begin to study the text and it will become clear. Is it Elizabethan? Is it Expressionistic? Realistic? The ideas of the play will be expressed through actions, and every action takes place in circumstances and a mood is created. The play will become clear as you study the text. Characters will emerge, and you will be able to see what class they come from. From the sequences, you can trace the plot and the development of the idea.

In the beginning, the script is outside you—a body of material that is external—but as you study, breaking it down into actions so that you can understand the growth of the playwright's idea, you begin to take it inside yourself.

Stage 2: Lifting the Idea

As soon as you can lift the idea and words from the page, you are in the second stage of rehearsal. At this stage, especially, you must guard against the temptation to memorize, for memorization blocks real understanding. As the text becomes more familiar and you are awakened to the style, ideas, and the playwright's meaning, the words gradually belong to you.

Resort to the use of a thesaurus if you have difficulty in understanding some words.

The play must always be fresh to you. Don't bring in yesterday's rehearsal. Always leave yourself open and truthful. Never push. Relax; let the circumstances of the play feed you, and each time you will be able to perform anew, with true spontaneity.

Stage 3: Realizing the Play

When you are confident in the interpretation of your part and that it has helped the author in realizing the play, you have made your contribution to the play.

CHAPTER TWELVE

The Actor's Contribution

The theatre has in it the element of surprise. There is an audience waiting in the dark for the curtain to rise. The actor then has the occasion, through the use of his talent and technique, to keep his audience spellbound.

The purpose of the technique, which is so emphasized, is to keep the actor from those techniques that are outmoded, or that have been abused in the name of Stanislavski.

The text of the playwright is the only point from which the actor can conceivably start. He must approach the script with no prejudices or preconceived opinions. The study of the script should proceed as follows:

1. The actor must lose his dependency on the words and go to the actions of the play.
2. The actions come first and words second. Words come out of the action.

By reading the play several times carefully, the actor can explore every aspect of it. In the contemporary theatre one is led to believe that it is the proper role of the director alone to discover the play, passing along his interpretation to the actors in rehearsal. But the actor must also become deeply involved with the playwright, discovering why the play was written and how the actor's interpretation can add to what has been established by the director. The actor cannot properly perform this function without accepting his responsibility of personal involvement with the playwright. Together with the director they become aware of the style of the play.

To be "interdependent" with the director and other members of the cast in approaching the play, the actor brings his talent to the interpretation of the part.

Working backward from the text the actor then asks—when and where does the action take place? The present tense of the play leads to the past, as the words on the page lead to the subtext, to the unspoken thoughts of the characters.

The actor, through the deep understanding of the circumstances, creates the indispensable need for him to use his imagination. The nature of his imagination is to try to visualize, as completely as possible, the characters and circumstances of the place.

The larger circumstances of the play involve the actor in exploring the circumstances still further. There is the historical setting of the play, which must include the epoch, the country, the city, and the social situation, all of which reveal the play's epic size.

In the modern theatre the focus is on the characters and the human situation in which they find themselves. The author often deals with the division between two basic instincts of man.

1. His destructiveness when he deals solely with the appetites he was born with
2. His dissatisfied struggle to attain something higher in life than his instincts

This conflict is very epic and the actor must be prepared to deal with such themes.

One of the vital aspects of the actor's work is to find the universality and epic size of the playwright's ideas. The pull of the play is always toward some larger theme and the danger we fall into is making it small. The modern play questions life, questions what to do about it, questions how we must live. So the actor must get used to learning and dealing with critical problems that affect everyone—questions of love, loyalty and friendship, of family and children.

The purpose of this book is to give the actor a technique and to put him in touch with a craft that I consider to be a totality of heart, mind, and spirit—an art that liberates ideas, and in so doing transforms the actor into an instrument of artistic purpose. These goals are what a good American actor must strive for.

To be articulate about the author's ideas and to be effective in communicating them is the responsibility of the actor. He doesn't treat the ideas casually. He has to build them up so that they are universal. The ideas contain the truths that people have to live by. These truths are conveyed by the actor. In this form, he becomes an important member of society that contributes to the ongoing civilization.

ON MY WAY TO STANISLAVSKI

One day in 1925 I went to the New York Public Library to find some books on the theatre, on acting, on ideas. I sat very far from the other people, all of them engrossed in their work, studying and reading. I could see how large the room was, even though it was dimly lit. While sitting there, I noticed a young man sitting opposite me.

When I started to read, he unexpectedly said to me, "May I ask what you're interested . . . or what you're reading?" And I answered, "I'm interested in the theatre." A moment passed, and he said, "So am I!" Of course we both giggled, which put us at ease. As actors we immediately felt a bond between us. Whenever actors get together they feel this closeness.

As we spoke and he told me he was an actor, I said, "I thought so, and I think maybe I know you." He said, "Well, I know you!" (I had acted a lot.) I told him that I was interested in the ideas that were coming out of Europe. Because American actors were separated from Europe, they didn't have contact with European theatrical life and concepts and weren't aware of what was being done there with Realism or Post-Realism. I knew all this was going on, but getting hold of material was difficult.

I explained this to him, and he said to me, "I think there is someone in New York who is doing a play that would interest you. It's a production in a very small theatre." He gave me the name of the theatre and told me where it was.

The theatre was on the East Side in the lower twenties, in a tenement building, with small steps going up. To the left was a room—just a room—and that's where the production of *The Sea Woman's Cloak* was taking place. It was a small room, very dimly lit, with about fifteen chairs about. In the corner was a woman, very huddled up, in dark clothes, looking through what seemed to be opera glasses.

She was very interesting. There was nobody else there. Perhaps a few more people came in just before the play began. When the curtain went up, a miracle happened.

It was a brilliant production; brilliant, stimulating, interesting, aesthetically a joy—it was a poem! What was astonishing was that there were American actors acting with a grace, a knowledge, a style, and a security that I hadn't seen. I soon found out that this play was directed by Richard Boleslavski, a Russian director of fame, a director in the Moscow Art Theatre, which, for years, had been under the supervision of Konstantin Stanislavski. I knew this; I understood this; I knew almost immediately that this approach was what I was looking for. I found out that Boleslavski and the lady in the corner, Madame Maria Ouspenskaya, had come to America and started a theatre, or a laboratory. It was called the Laboratory Theatre, and it was for students who were interested in the Russian style of acting.

Within a day or two I had joined the Laboratory Theatre. Although I was acting at other theatres all the time, I stayed at the Laboratory Theatre for two years, where I attended lectures by Boleslavski, movement classes with Mordkin, and voice classes and some technique classes with Madame Ouspenskaya. It was a small conservatory, and Boleslavski was doing rehearsals and productions. I watched his rehearsals, and took part in some of the plays.

My life went on. I acted, helped enormously by the ideas that were introduced there about the theatre, about acting, about the actor in the theatre, and the importance of the actor. All this came through with great, great honesty, and I was profoundly influenced by what Boleslavski gave to his audiences.

Time passed and I continued acting in the theatre. I had the habit of going to Europe when I had the time, the freedom, and the money. At one point I was in Paris, and Harold Clurman was there at the same time.

Harold had initiated the Group Theatre, of which I was a part. To me he was a savior; he had made a theatre to which I wanted to belong. He had seen me act and asked me to join, so I did. Harold was the man who did the most to open up my talent and my mind, who helped me educate myself about plays. He had significance in my life, in my theatrical life.

In Paris, Harold said to me, "You know, Stella, Stanislavski is here." By this time, I had heard a great deal about Stanislavski. I had known people who were participating in the Stanislavski technique. I myself was part of the Group Theatre, where the technique was supposedly being used. But as an actress who had had a great deal of experience elsewhere, I resented acting with some of the principles that were used at the Group Threatre. Because of this, I became a stranger. I excluded myself from the way in which they rehearsed, and the way the plays were directed. All this was known to everyone. They knew that I was against what was happening at the Group Theatre.

Harold also knew my feelings about the Group Theatre. He thought it was a good idea for me to meet Mr. Stanislavski.

But I was hesitant. The idea frightened me, because I said to Harold, "If I meet him, I will have in me a sense that he was represented at the Group Theatre in a way I didn't want."

In the end I went with Harold Clurman to Mr. Stanislavski's home. It was a small French apartment with a small French elevator. When Harold opened the door, there were a few people in the room. It was a small room, and in the far corner was Stanislavski. The moment of meeting him was such a shock to me that I stood and didn't move. Harold went over and greeted him. With Stanislavski were his doctor, a friend, and Madame Chekhova. Madame Chekhova stood near the door with me and said, "You must go over and shake Mr. Stanislavski's hand." I looked at her and said, "No." She said, "You must." I said, "No, I mustn't," and I didn't. I stood, completely unable to move, forward or backward. I was paralyzed by the whole moment.

Within a short time Mr. Stanislavski and the others suggested that we all go to the Champs-Élysees. When we got there, Mr. Stanislavski sat on a bench against a tree, and we sat around him. There was great laughter and gaiety—the intimacy and wittiness that actors have. I remember distinctly Stanislavski chiding Madame Chekhova and calling her a ham, and of course she laughed. He pretended to bully her, and she pretended to be stronger than he was. There was humor, and an absolute moment of ensemble, and the joy of being there.

Mr. Stanislavski spoke to everyone, and he perceived that I was reticent. Naturally, he would notice that, because he had the "eye" and nothing got past him. He finally turned to me and said, "Young lady, everybody has spoken to me but you." That was the moment that I looked at him, eye to eye, we were together. I heard myself saying, "Mr. Stanislavski, I loved the theatre until you came along, and now I hate it!" He looked at me a little longer, and then he said, "Well, then you must come to see me tomorrow."

That was probably the moment that I remember best. We said good-bye, and I went to see Mr. Stanislavski the next day.

I thought it was important for me to bring somebody in case I did not understand him. The friend that I brought was a great help. Sitting with Mr. Stanislavski, I found out that we could speak quite easily in French. He asked me many questions. I told him that I was very unhappy about a play that I was in at that time called *The Gentle Woman* by Don Powell. I told him that I failed in certain moments of the play when I could neither continue the character nor understand how to continue the character. He was terribly intrigued, and we worked on the concept of the character. Within a minute or two I realized he was very interested in me as an actress. He wanted me to resolve my problem. Here was the one man in the world who could help! And so I opened up my whole heart to him.

I told him that I was a practiced actress. He knew of my family: He knew because my father, Jacob P. Adler, had produced *The Living Corpse* by Leo Tolstoi before he, Stanislavski, had played it. Adler was the first one in the world to play it, and this, of course, was known by everyone. Stanislavski understood that I was the daughter of Jacob P. Adler and Sara Adler, a theatrical family.

Stanislavski and I were in the greatest closeness of director and actress, and very soon it was just actor and actress! We worked together every day for many, many weeks. In those periods, there were certain things that he asked me to do. Particularly, he made very clear to me that an actor must have an enormous imagination that is free and not inhibited by self-consciousness. I understood that he was very much an actor who was fed by the imagination. He explained to me how important it was to use the imagination on the stage. He then explained in detail how important it was to use the circumstances. He said that *where* you are is what you are, and how you are, and what you can be. You are in a place that will feed you, that will give you strength, that will give you the ability to do whatever you want.

He asked me to use the circumstances. He said, "Just do a few things and put a plot around it." I was fluent (maybe too fluent!) I said, "Yes." I went to the window and I was devastated, because imaginatively I saw something in which I was emotionally, immediately involved. Then I walked over to the desk and wrote my name at the bottom of the letter. Again, I was dramatically, deeply involved with the plot, and I knew there was only one more thing to do; that was to get my hat and coat and leave the place.

These exercises can be done on any level. I took the dramatic level. It was closer to me, as I was a dramatic actress.

Mr. Stanislavski also told me—very much actor to actress—how he had suffered when he played *An Enemy of the People*. He said that he was a complete disaster. He didn't know the part; he didn't know where to touch it. He said it was difficult for him; that Ibsen was difficult for him. He told me that it took him ten years to find the part. While he was gathering the elements for a technique that would make acting easier, he found the answer to the problem that he had essentially experienced as an actor throughout his life, especially while working on *An Enemy of the People*. In this particular play, Stanislavski said that he had talked to the people and asked them to do something. That was wrong. He said, "I had to speak to the *soul* of the people. If I could reach their souls, I could get somewhere." Ten years after Stanislavski had originally played the role, the play was revived; the part was his and he was then able to play it.

We worked intimately on scenes and on improvisations, and I was able to be completely at ease, completely at home. I felt as if I had worked with him for a lifetime. He was gentle and "absolutely theatre"; nothing but theatre came through. Kindness and interest—a master with a student.

He couldn't see me in the mornings, because he said he had speech difficulties—that he was inclined to lisp. So he would practice every morning for two hours. I laughed at him, and he laughed at himself.

After many weeks, he told me that he had come to Paris to see his family, but that I hadn't let him do that, and would I give him some time to be with them? Of course I said yes, and I thanked him, said good-bye, and left.

But the next morning I called him and said, "Mr. Stanislavski, we did not cover some element of the technique," explaining that there was something he had not made clear. He said, "Come right over!" (By this time my notes were voluminous!)

When I did walk away from Stanislavski's apartment, I wandered the streets of Paris. I knew Paris; I knew it as any fervent actress would, who looks at the roofs, at every doorknob, at every little shop. I was infatuated with Paris. I had worked with the master teacher of the world, the man whose words were going to flood the world with truth. That sense he had, of how truthful you had to be; this was his heritage, this is what he gave away. I could never thank him enough. I remember walking down the street and saying, "Mr. Stanislavski, I can't thank you personally, but all my life I will dedicate myself to other people, to give them what you have given me."

Suggested Scenes and Characters to Study and Work On

ALL MY SONS
by Arthur Miller
Ann and Chris, End of Act I

CAT ON A HOT TIN ROOF
by Tennessee Williams
Maggie and Brick, Act I, Scene 1

CAT ON A HOT TIN ROOF
by Tennessee Williams
Big Daddy and Brick, Act II

CHILDREN'S HOUR
by Lillian Hellman
Karen and Martha, Act III, Scene 1

COME BACK, LITTLE SHEBA
by William Inge
Doc and Lola, Act II, Scene 3

COME BACK, LITTLE SHEBA
by William Inge
Turk and Marie

CRUCIBLE
by Arthur Miller
Abigail and Proctor, forest scene

DARK AT THE TOP OF THE STAIRS
by William Inge
Rubin and Cora

DEATH OF A SALESMAN
by Arthur Miller
Linda's last monologue
(Requiem)

DEATH OF A SALESMAN
by Arthur Miller
Biff and Happy, Act I

DEATH OF BESSIE SMITH
by Edward Albee
Nurse and Orderly, Scene 4
Nurse and Intern, Scene 6

A DOLL'S HOUSE
by Henrik Ibsen
Torvald and Nora, Act I, Scene 1; End of Act III

GLASS MENAGERIE
by Tennessee Williams
Amanda and Laura, Act I, Scene 2
Laura and Jim, Act II, Scene 8

GOLDEN BOY
by Clifford Odets
Lorna and Joe, Act II, Scene 2

A HATFUL OF RAIN
by Michael Gazzo
Polo and Johnny, Act II
Father and Johnny, Act II, Scene 2

LOOK BACK IN ANGER
by John Osborne
Two Women

MADWOMAN OF CHAILLOT
by Jean Giraudoux
Three Women, Act II

ORPHEUS DESCENDING
by Tennessee Williams
Val and Carol, Act I
Lady and Val, Act II

OUR TOWN
by Thornton Wilder
George and Emily, Act II

PICNIC
by William Inge
Madge and Hal, end of Act II
Rosemary and Howard

RAINMAKER
by N. Richard Nash
Lizzie and File, Act II
Lizzie and Starbuck, end of Act II

A STREETCAR NAMED DESIRE
by Tennessee Williams
Blanch and Stanley, Act I, Scene 2
                    Act III, Scene 4
Stella and Stanley, Act I, Scene 2
                    Act III, Scene 1
Blanche and Mitch, Act II, Scene 2
                    Act III, Scene 3

SUMMER AND SMOKE
by Tennessee Williams
Alma and John
Alma and Salesman

TIME OF YOUR LIFE
by William Saroyan
Joe and Mary, Act II

27 WAGONS FULL OF COTTON
by Tennessee Williams
Vicarro and Flora, Scene 2

A VIEW FROM THE BRIDGE
by Arthur Miller
Catherine and Rodolfo
Eddie and Mr. Alfieri, Act I

WAITING FOR LEFTY
by Clifford Odets
Joe and Edna, Scene 1

ZOO STORY
by Edward Albee
Peter and Jerry
"I've been to the zoo . . ."

Biography of
Stella Adler

Born in New York City, Stella Adler is the youngest daughter of Jacob P. and Sarah Adler, the foremost tragedians of the Yiddish stage in America. Jacob P. Adler, internationally called "the Jewish Henry Irving," presented a classical repertory of unusual quality at his Yiddish Arts Company, and according to most theatre historians, the Yiddish American theatre flourished at the turn of the century due to the contributions of the Adler family.

It was said that "no curtain in New York went up without an Adler behind it," and in 1939, at the time of Sarah Adler's fiftieth anniversary debut on the American-Jewish stage, there were no less than seventeen family members active in the theatre. All of Stella's immediate family—including her brother Luther—became actors. In Stella's words, "In my family, immediately, when you could barely walk, you were put on the stage."

Stella Adler made her stage debut in 1906 at the age of four in her father's production of *Broken Hearts* at the Grand Street Theatre in New York. Another memory for her was playing the part of a pageboy in *The Merchant of Venice*. The following year Stella took the part of one of the young princes in *Richard III*. For the next ten years she acted with her parents both here and abroad in a variety of roles from the plays of Ibsen, Tolstoy, Hauptmann, Shakespeare, and other classics.

In the winter of 1919 Stella made her London debut at the Pavilion as Naomi in *Elisa Ben Avia*. Upon her return to New York she accepted featured roles in several commercial productions. Billed as "Lola" Adler, she made her first Broadway appearance as the Butterfly (Apatura Clythia) in *The World We Live In* ("The Insect Comedy"), Karel Čapek's smash hit of the 1922–23 theatrical season.

Stella Adler attended New York University and later studied at the American Laboratory Theatre. There she came in contact with Stanislavski's new approach to acting as taught by two of his most important disciples, Maria Ouspenskaya and Richard Boleslavski. It was considered by far the soundest creative technique for actors, and Stella put this technique to good use in a number of important Lab productions. She first appeared as Baroness Crème de la Crème in *Straw Hat*, now billed as "Stella Adler," and she has used her real name ever since. Her two other most notable roles with the Lab were as Elly in *The Big Lake* and as Beatrice in *Much Ado About Nothing*.

From 1927 to 1931 Stella Adler starred in more than one hundred plays. She spent two seasons at the Irving Place Theatre with Jacob Ben Ami, a well-known Yiddish actor. She also toured Latin America, Western Europe, and throughout the United States with a repertory company. Back in New York in 1930, Stella returned to her father's company for a series of leading parts in *The God of Vengeance, The Lower Depths, Liliom, The Witch of Castile*, and *Jew Süss*.

The spring of 1931 marks the point at which Stella Adler joined the struggling Group Theatre, initiated by former Theatre Guild member, Harold Clurman (later Stella's husband). John Gassner wrote in *Theatre of Our Times* that he considered the Group "a memory of the best ensemble acting Broadway has ever known."

The Group Theatre members were socially conscious visionaries who sought to provide a depression-era alternative to commercial theatre. "After analyzing, dissecting, and reshaping the theatre," Stella remembers, "two ideas emerged . . . the first idea asked the actor to become aware of himself (the individual actor's total personality was supposed to be dealt with) . . . the second idea talked of the actor in relation to his craft. . . . When these two ideas merged, the actor realized that this theatre demanded a basic understanding of a complex artistic principle: that all people connected with this theatre, the actor, designer, playwright, director, etc., had of necessity to arrive at a single point of view which the theme of the play also expressed."

This credo that inspired the creative collective proved itself in the manifestation of the first Group production, Paul Green's *The House of Connelly* in which Stella played Geraldine Connelly. Brooks Atkinson of *The New York Times* reflected the sentiments of nearly all the critics: "Their group performance is too beautifully imagined and modulated to concentrate on personal achievements. There is not a gaudy, brittle or facile stroke in their acting. . . . It is not too much to hope that something fine and true has been started in the American theatre."

Atkinson proved prophetic: The Group Theatre never fell below the standard it first established for itself, even producing from its ranks one of America's foremost playwrights, Clifford Odets.

For the Group's follow-up, and in accordance with their no-star policy, Stella accepted a small part in *1931*, Paul and Claire Sifton's statement on the depression-era jobless. The completion of the first New York season was Maxwell Anderson's *Night over Taos*, with Stella as Dona Josepha.

Success Story opened the Group's second season, and Stella's performance as Sarah Glassman, a jilted secretary, attracted attention from the theatrical community. Group compatriot Robert Lewis recalls in his *Slings and Arrows* that many well-known actors (Noel Coward and Ruth Chatterton, among others) would stop in nightly to study Stella in the final scene of the play.

Stella continued performing leading roles in *The Big Night* as Myra Bonney, in *Hilda Cassidy* as Hilda, and in *Gentlewoman* as Gwyn Ballantine.

After *Gentlewoman*, dissatisfied with her performance and disturbed by director Lee Strasberg's excessive use of "affective memory" exercises, Stella took a leave of absence from the Group and went to Europe. There she was introduced by Olga Knipper (Moscow Art Theatre star and widow of Anton Chekhov) to Konstantin Stanislavski himself. In response to Stella's complaint that certain aspects of Stanislavski's system frustrated her, Stanislavski suggested that perhaps she did not use it properly, and he offered to coach her personally.

For the next five weeks Stella and Stanislavski worked daily on a scene she had found difficult in *Gentlewoman*. As a result of this, she was, upon her return, able to correct the Group Theatre's interpretation of Stanislavski with a formal report to her fellow actors, complete with charts outlining the system and the blunt admonition that the undue emphasis on "affective memory" warped the actor.

Also that summer Stella herself began to give classes. One of her first students, Margaret Barker, needed coaching for the Group's production of *The Case of Clyde Griffiths*. Foster Hirsch later quoted Ms. Barker's assessment of the experience: "In a half hour working with Stella Adler on that play I knew more about it than from all the rehearsals."

Stella returned to acting in Group productions in 1934 when she portrayed flamboyant actress Adah Menken in *Gold Eagle Guy*. Her interpretation of Bessie Berger in Odets's *Awake and Sing* (1935) again excited the critics. Robert Lewis recalls that Stella "set a standard for Jewish-mother parts that has not been approached since; omitting the usual self-pity and leavening the dominating nature of the woman with lofty humor."

After Stella's final stage appearance with the Group as Clara in *Paradise Lost* (1935), she headed for Hollywood. She debuted in *Love on Toast* as Stella "Ardler"—"the producers decided they needed a 'goyishe' name for the marquee," she remarked. She still returned to the Group Theatre, primarily to direct. It was Stella who staged the acclaimed touring production of *Golden Boy* in 1938.

Stella felt her teaching vocation strongly by 1940. She developed the Dramatic Workshop at the New School for Social Research and taught for two years there.

In 1941, the year of the Group Theatre's dissolution, Ms. Adler appeared in her second film, *Shadow of the Thin Man* (she would go on to appear in a third, *My Girl Tisa,* in 1948). She later spent time behind the scenes as associate producer to Arthur Freed at MGM on films *DuBarry Was a Lady, Madame Curie,* and also *For Me and My Gal,* among other Judy Garland films. Stella insisted that the studio heads nurture Judy Garland's talent and not squander her gift on unchallenging parts.

Broadway called Stella back to the stage, however, in May of 1943, when she played Catherine Canrick in Max Reinhardt's stunning production of *Sons and Soldiers*. Later that year she staged *Manhattan Nocturne*.

She went on to direct well-received performances of *Polonaise,* a historical extravaganza set to the music of Chopin, in 1945, *Sunday Breakfast* in 1952, and the antiwar musical *Johnny Johnson* in 1956. Broadway was deprived of her landmark production of *Alice in Wonderland* when the potential producers demanded that she recast the lead with a bankable star. Stella Adler's integrity ruled out that option and she declined. Nonetheless, the show ran with great success off Broadway for quite some time.

Stella Adler has always been a vivid and colorful performer, and audiences were rewarded when the grand dame of the American theatre delivered larger-than-life performances as Clothilde Hilyard in Claiborne Foster's *Pretty Little Parlor* in 1944, and as Zinadia, the lion tamer, in a Theatre Guild revival of Leonid Andreyev's *He Who Gets Slapped.* Stella Adler's final stage appearance was in London in 1961 as Madame Rosepetal in Arthur Kopit's *Oh Dad, Poor Dad, Mama's Hung You in the Closet and I'm Feelin' So Sad.* In her acting career she appeared in more than 200 productions.

In addition to her performances, Stella Adler's greatest gift to the American theatrical tradition is undoubtedly her educating thousands of actors from the time the doors of her Stella Adler Acting Studio opened in 1949. "In our time in history, there are no standards for the actor. All formal rules for the actor have changed: his behavior, his clothing, his speech, etc. The teacher knows that each actor is different, and a talent may lie dormant. The actor of our time has to be helped," Ms. Adler has said.

She designed a comprehensive two-year program with special attention given to play analysis and characterization. By 1960 Stella Adler's studio, now renamed the Stella Adler Conservatory of Acting, had grown to include more than a dozen faculty members. She continued personally to teach master classes in acting and script interpretation. She also served as adjunct professor of acting at Yale University's School of Drama in 1966–67, and she has been associated with New York University for many years. The Stella Adler Conservatory of Acting West opened in Los Angeles in 1986. For her experience and contribution to the acting community, she has been honored by the New School of Social Research with a Doctor of Humane Letters degree, and with a Doctor of Fine Arts degree from Smith College.

Today Stella Adler continues to guide her students through the actor's quest. Anyone who has observed Stella's classes in New York and Los Angeles knows that she keeps ever-present what Konstantin Stanislavski taught her: "The source of acting is imagination and the key to its problems is truth, truth in the circumstances of the play." She inspires her pupils to make the ideas of the playwright understandable. She asks them—as she does—to equate acting with life itself: "Creating and interpreting means total involvement, the totality of heart, mind, and spirit."

—Compiled by Irene Gilbert